Nothing But the Truth

A Life Style of Christian Integrity

Nothing But the Truth

A Life Style of
Christian Integrity

John W. Stevenson

Destiny Image Publishers
P.O. Box 310
Shippensburg, PA 17257

"Speaking to the Purposes of God
for this Generation and
for the Generations to Come"

ISBN 1-56043-121-0

For Worldwide Distribution
Printed in the U.S.A.

Destiny Image books are available through these fine distributors outside the United States:

Christian Growth, Inc. Jalan Kilang-Timor, Singapore 0315	Successful Christian Living Capetown, Rep. of South Africa
Lifestream Nottingham, England	Vision Resources Ponsonby, Auckland, New Zealand
Rhema Ministries Trading Randburg, South Africa	WA Buchanan Company Geebung, Queensland, Australia
Salvation Book Centre Petaling, Jaya, Malaysia	Word Alive Niverville, Manitoba, Canada

Dedication

This book is dedicated to You, Lord Jesus. May it accomplish in Your Body what You have purposed it to do. I will always serve You and love You. Thank You for entrusting me with this revelation on truth. Give me the grace to walk out the contents of this book. My heart is Your throne!

Acknowledgments

With much gratitude I acknowledge the following people: my wonderful wife Marissa, whom I have found to truly be the woman spoken of in Proverbs 31. I will always love you. My children, John, Leslie, Nicholas, David, and Christopher, who continue to bring joy to my life. Raymond and Patricia Stevenson, my parents who raised me and introduced me to the love of God. Paul and Ernestine Menefield, who gave me a wonderful wife and whom I have found to be wonderful in-laws. Pastor C. Edward Linville, for giving me the opportunity to share in his ministry and to bring forth this teaching on truth. Dr. Michael E. and Carol Dantley, senior pastors of Christ Emmanuel Christian Fellowship, for giving Marissa and I the opportunity to share in the vision God has given them. They are wonderful friends and a blessing to us both. The pastors, staff, and church family at Christ Emmanuel, their love, prayer, and support are an encouragement to us. Let's pray that we all will walk out the contents of this book. Kelley Varner, senior pastor of Praise Tabernacle Ministries, for writing such a powerful foreword and for always being an example of truth to me. Lafayette Scales, senior pastor of Rhema Christian Center, for his thoughts and comments concerning this topic. Gwen Steward and Juanita Brightwell, for their prayers during the writing of this book and for taking time to review the manuscript. Melissa Moody, my Ministry Assistant, who spent hours upon hours working with me to make sure nothing was left out or was unclear in this book. Having you to work with, Melissa, is a tremendous blessing. Your dedication and commitment will not go unrewarded; thank you. Don Nori and the staff at Destiny Image, for following hard after the Lord.

Contents

Foreword

Truth is reality. As we continue to walk into the 90s, lines of demarcation are being clearly drawn. We are witnessing a global polarization. Our Lord in His parables called it the maturing of the wheat and the tares.

There are two kinds of people on this planet: the faithful followers of the One who is the Truth (Jn. 14:6), and those who are madly pursuing vanity and folly. The King and His Kingdom belong to that which is permanent; all else is passing away.

Simply, there are but two men on earth: Adam and Christ. Both are a family, an army, a people, and a nation. Adam is after the flesh and is "the lie." Christ is after the Spirit and is "the truth" (1 Jn.

2:27). Every man is dominated by one of these two natures.

John Stevenson is a man of the Spirit. He is a gifted prophetic psalmist to the Body of Christ, and now an author. I have ministered with John, and he and his lovely wife Marissa have been in my home. They have a real heart for the Lord and are being raised up to speak the truth in love.

In *Nothing But the Truth* John lays this foundation stone clearly and forthrightly. His exegesis on this Bible subject is sound and easy to follow. He begins by beseeching us, individually and corporately, to be honest. Once our motives are pure, we are exhorted to be filled with the Holy Ghost, the Spirit of Truth. Only then can we declare the Word of the Lord with genuine power. All that we speak must be based on His Word. This operation of the Word, anointed by the Spirit, will bring about the transformation of our hearts and the renewing of our minds. This change will bring challenge, but having passed the test, we will become the glorious Church, walking in the way of Truth!

There is hope for America and the world. Every lie is being burned with fire in the Day of the Lord. The Church is waking up. Arise! Eat the Word! You will become a lover of Truth!

Kelley Varner, Th.B., D.D.
Senior Pastor, Praise Tabernacle
Richlands, North Carolina

Introduction

For some time now God has been dealing with my heart concerning the operation of truth. No doubt He has been dealing with you as well, or you would not be reading this introduction. There is something very fundamental and foundational to our Christian walk that has been lost in our quest for the "more spiritual" things. That main ingredient is *truth*. Because we have not kept truth in its proper place, the foundation that the Church has built upon in recent years has begun to crumble, and the integrity and character of the Church, the Body of Christ, is being destroyed.

The word for truth in the Greek is *alētheia*. It means "the unveiled reality lying at the basis of and agreeing with appearance" (#225 Strong's). Before submitting our lives to the lordship of Jesus Christ, truth was not a major priority. Most people just say what is comfortable or convenient. Much of today's society is built on lies and deceit. People are paid large sums of money to create illusions. That's one of the major problems with advertising. What you see is not always what you get. Things are made to look better than they really are. The world's train of thought is, "What you don't know, won't hurt you!" That's not *true*! What you don't know can kill you! If you don't know that a fallen electrical wire may be charged with thousands of volts of electricity and you pick it up, it will kill you! The world has no problem with holding back the truth. In a very subtle way, we ourselves, as believers, have started to disregard truth also.

Have you ever received a call from a bill collector and promised payment, knowing that you did not have the means to pay? Or better yet, did you tell the person it was in the mail, all the while knowing you hadn't sent it yet? Then you got off the phone and asked God to help you to meet that commitment. Now this is a simple illustration, but it's serious. First, you lied. Second, God can not and will not support or endorse a lie. Therefore, when the money doesn't come, it's not that God wants to hold out on you, it's that the words you may have spoken and called faith or believing God, He considered lies.

There are times when God would have us speak in faith concerning a situation, but it's supposed to be the Holy Spirit guiding us and not you or I speaking and expecting God to come to our rescue.

Once we have accepted Jesus as our Lord, we must also recognize that our old practices and ways must be submitted to Him—even simple lies like the one illustrated. Jesus said, "I am the way, *the truth,* and the life" (Jn. 14:6). When we chose Jesus, we chose *truth—the way of truth.*

The way of truth is the way of holiness discussed in Isaiah 35:8-10.

And an highway shall be there, and a way, and it shall be called The way of holiness; the unclean shall not pass over it; but it shall be for those: the wayfaring men, though fools, shall not err therein. No lion shall be there, nor any ravenous beast shall go up thereon, it shall not be found there; but the redeemed shall walk there: and the ransomed of the Lord shall return, and come to Zion with songs and everlasting joy upon their heads: they shall obtain joy and gladness, and sorrow and sighing shall flee away.

It is through truth that we walk in holiness. It is by accepting the truth that we can make changes that produce a consistency in our walk. The way of truth is the place where the redeemed walk.

The way of truth is the *path* Jesus talks about in Matthew 7:13-14.

Enter ye in at the strait gate: for wide is the gate, and broad is the way, that leadeth to destruction, and many there be which go in thereat: because strait is the gate, and narrow is the way, which leadeth unto life, and few there be that find it.

The ways of the world are broad, with a mindset of "anything goes," but the way of truth is narrow. The world says, "Do it your way." The way of truth is *His* way. Not too many are willing to walk in this narrow way, yet God requires it from His Body.

The way of truth is the place of *protection* mentioned in Psalm 91.

He that dwelleth in the secret place of the most High shall abide under the shadow of the Almighty. I will say of the Lord, He is my refuge and my fortress: my God; in Him will I trust. Surely He shall deliver thee from the snare of the fowler, and from the noisome pestilence. He shall cover thee with His feathers, and under His wings shalt thou trust: His truth shall be thy shield and buckler. (Psalm 91:1-4)

The word *buckler* in Hebrew is *cocherah.* It means "something surrounding the person" (#5507 Strong's). Truth protects on all sides at all times.

The way of truth is the *process* talked about in First Corinthians 13:11-12.

When I was a child, I spake as a child, I understood as a child, I thought as a child: but when I became a man, I put away childish things. For now we see through a glass, darkly; but then face to face: now I know in part; but then shall I know even as also I am known.

The way of truth is a process that brings us to a place of maturity. In order to become a man, a mature person, we must accept truth. It is truth, God's Word, that brings things into the light and causes us to come "face to face" with ourselves and the Lord.

We are changed as we are willing to accept the truth. The Body of Christ is not maturing because we have not kept truth as our foundation. Many are walking around held captive by the fear of what others will think if they tell the truth. Yet Ephesians 4:15 says, "But speaking the truth in love, may grow up into Him in all things... ."

It is by the Spirit of truth ruling in our hearts that we are able to walk in truth. It is the Spirit of truth who helps us to accept the truth about ourselves. Truth works in many ways and if the Body of Christ intends to change the world in which it lives, every member must allow truth to be their gauge for everything.

Many are rejecting truth. We have no idea of the devastating results that could be awaiting all of us because of this rejection. In this book I want to talk about what truth wants to accomplish and what it should be accomplishing in the Body of Christ. Many people in the Body are walking around in deception. This book is intended to help all of us get back on course and start moving in the right direction.

The Church is moving into the Third Day, leaving the Inner Court and moving to the Most Holy Place. We're moving from sonship to heirs—joint heirs with Jesus. We're leaving the mixture and mingling of flesh and spirit for the complete and awesome presence of God, where we know even as we are known (1 Cor. 13:12) and we behold His glory full of grace and *truth* (Jn. 1:14). We must ask the Lord to help us remove our masks and to give us the courage to enter into the place He intended for us to walk—*the way of truth.*

Chapter One

It's Time to Tell the Truth

Do not lie to each other, since you have taken off your old self with its practices and have put on the new self, which is being renewed in knowledge in the image of its Creator. (Colossians 3:9-10 NIV)

Have you ever wondered why it's sometimes harder to tell the truth and much easier to tell a lie? It's one of the characteristics of a life not yielded to the total lordship of the Lord Jesus Christ. It is only by the power of the Holy Spirit and the appropriation of God's Word in our lives that we can walk consistently in the truth. As members of the Body of Christ, we must recognize that God speaks very specifically about truth and the consequences of lying. In Proverbs 6, the writer named seven things that are an abomination to the Lord. One of those things is "a lying tongue."

*These six things doth the Lord hate: yea, seven are an abomination unto Him: a proud look, **a lying tongue**, and hands that shed innocent blood, an heart that deviseth wicked imaginations, feet that be swift in running to mischief, **a false witness that speaketh lies**, and he that soweth discord among brethren.* (Proverbs 6:16-19)

Notice that not only in verse 17 does he say "a lying tongue," but in verse 19 he says, "a false witness that speaks lies." In Matthew 26:59-61 we read that the chief priests and elders sought out false witnesses so they could put Jesus Christ to death. At first they could find no reason, but then two false witnesses came and gave the religious leaders what they wanted.

Now the chief priests, and elders, and all the council, sought false witness against Jesus, to put Him to death; But found none: yea, though many false witnesses came, yet found they none. At the last came two false witnesses. (Matthew 26:59-60)

We can also see that satan used the same scheme in Acts 6:8-14 to kill Stephen.

And Stephen, full of faith and power, did great wonders and miracles among the people. Then there arose certain of the synagogue, which is called the synagogue of the Libertines, and Cyrenians, and Alexandrians, and of them of Cilicia and of Asia, disputing with Stephen. And they were not able to resist the wisdom and the spirit by which he spake. Then they suborned men, which said, We have heard him speak blasphemous words against Moses, and against God. And they stirred up the people, and the elders, and the scribes, and came upon him, and caught him, and brought him to the council, And set up false witnesses, which said, This man ceaseth not to speak blasphemous words against this holy place, and the law: for we have heard him say, that this Jesus of

Nazareth shall destroy this place, and shall change the customs which Moses delivered us.

The religious leaders set up false witnesses against him. The devil is still using this same tactic in the Church today. Once a ministry begins to grow or a leader is being used by God in a mighty way, you can always look for false accusations. Unfortunately, the tragedy we must address is very often that the attack does not come from outside the Church, but the inside. More often than not, it comes from a religious spirit, or a spirit of tradition. God's anger is kindled against those who raise false accusations. It will be judged!

In these scriptural accounts false witnesses were sought out, but we must also be willing to see that when we engage in gossip or conversations that are speculation and not fact, we are many times joining in false accusations. It happens very subtly with statements like, "Did you hear...?" or "I heard..." or even "I was talking to brother so-and-so and he said...." I think you can see my point. That's how false accusations get started. However, if we will let Him, the Holy Spirit will help us be sensitive in this area.

In Acts 5:1-11, we see the consequences of lying in the early Church.

But a certain man named Ananias, with Sapphira his wife, sold a possession, and kept back part of the price, his wife being privy to it, and brought a certain part, and laid it at the apostles' feet. But Peter said, Ananias, why hath Satan filled thine heart to lie to the Holy Ghost, and to keep back part of the price of the land? Whiles it remained, was it not thine own? and after it was sold, was it not in thine own power? why hast thou conceived this thing in thine heart? thou hast not lied unto men, but unto God. (Acts 5:1-4)

Notice that what Peter mentioned here was Ananias' heart. That was the problem. It starts with the heart. Only God knows the heart of every man. That's why it's important to allow the Holy Spirit access into your every part. Jeremiah 17:9-10 makes very clear the state of a man's heart:

The heart is deceitful above all things, and desperately wicked: who can know it? I the Lord search the heart, I try the reins, even to give every man according to his ways, and according to the fruit of his doings.

God desires truth in the inward parts.

Behold, Thou desirest truth in the inward parts: and in the hidden part Thou shalt make me to know wisdom. (Psalm 51:6)

It says, "in the hidden part Thou shalt make me to know wisdom." Wisdom is knowledge properly applied to a situation. God gives us knowledge concerning the hidden things in our hearts. It is wisdom when we respond appropriately to what was revealed. Ananias thought he could hide something from God, but nothing is hidden from Him.

> *And Ananias hearing these words fell down, and gave up the ghost: and great fear came on all them that heard these things. And the young men arose, wound him up, and carried him out, and buried him. And it was about the space of three hours after, when his wife, not knowing what was done, came in. And Peter answered unto her, Tell me whether ye sold the land for so much? And she said, Yea, for so much. Then Peter said unto her, How is it that ye have agreed together to tempt the Spirit of the Lord? behold, the feet of them which have buried thy husband are at the door, and shall carry thee out. Then fell she down straightway at his feet, and yielded up the ghost: and the young men came in, and found her dead, and, carrying her forth, buried her by her husband. And great fear came upon all the church, and upon as many as heard these things. (Acts 5:5-11)*

Even as the Church was starting, we see that satan was there. Notice what Peter said to Ananias in verse 3: "Why hath *Satan* filled thine heart to lie to the Holy Ghost?" Peter immediately exposed the source of the lie: satan. Not only did Peter confront

Ananias, he also let him know that Ananias did not lie to him, Peter, but to the Holy Ghost! He told Ananias in verse 4: "Thou hast not lied unto men, but unto God." You may be asking yourself, "Why isn't this happening in the Church today when someone lies?" There's a good reason: The Church today is not the Church of Acts. Over the years truth has been watered down. What used to be black and white is now gray, and what used to be right and wrong is now reasoned away for a more common ground. That ground is called *compromise*. Lying in any form is not a part of the Kingdom of God, and if the truth be known, all liars will be destroyed.

In Revelation 21:8 it lists those who will have their place in the lake of fire. The last ones John mentioned are all liars:

But the fearful, and unbelieving, and the abominable, and murderers, and whoremongers, and sorcerers, and idolaters, and all liars, shall have their part in the lake which burneth with fire and brimstone: which is the second death.

In order to understand God's severe penalty, you must realize where the problem started! It started in the heavens with lucifer. Lucifer was created by God. He had the honor and privilege of leading the heavenly host in worship, but something went wrong. It went wrong when he exalted himself.

How art thou fallen from heaven, O Lucifer, son of the morning! how art thou cut down to the ground, which didst weaken the nations! For thou hast said in thine heart, I will ascend into heaven, I will exalt my throne above the stars of God: I will sit also upon the mount of the congregation, in the sides of the north: I will ascend above the heights of the clouds; I will be like the most High. Yet thou shalt be brought down to hell, to the sides of the pit. (Isaiah 14:12-15)

The Scriptures tell us in Ezekiel 28:12-19 that lucifer was perfect in his ways until *iniquity* was found in his heart.

*Son of man, take up a lamentation upon the king of Tyrus, and say unto him, Thus saith the Lord God; Thou sealest up the sum, full of wisdom, and perfect in beauty. Thou hast been in Eden the garden of God; every precious stone was thy covering, the sardius, topaz, and the diamond, the beryl, the onyx, and the jasper, the sapphire, the emerald, and the carbuncle, and gold: the workmanship of thy tabrets and of thy pipes was prepared in thee in the day that thou wast created. Thou art the anointed cherub that covereth; and I have set thee so: thou wast upon the holy mountain of God; thou hast walked up and down in the midst of the stones of fire. **Thou wast perfect in thy ways** *from the day that thou wast created, till iniquity was found in thee.* (Ezekiel 28:12-15)

The following verses show the effects of iniquity. We are seeing it even today!

By the multitude of thy merchandise they have filled the midst of thee with violence, and thou hast sinned: therefore I will cast thee as profane out of the mountain of God: and I will destroy thee, O covering cherub, from the midst of the stones of fire. **Thine heart was lifted up because of thy beauty, thou hast corrupted thy wisdom by reason of thy brightness: I will cast thee to the ground, I will lay thee before kings, that they may behold thee.** *Thou hast defiled thy sanctuaries by the multitude of thine iniquities, by the iniquity of thy traffick;* **therefore will I bring forth a fire from the midst of thee, it shall devour thee, and I will bring thee to ashes upon the earth in the sight of all them that behold thee. All they that know thee among the people shall be astonished at thee: thou shalt be a terror, and never shalt thou be any more.** (Ezekiel 28:16-19)

A word for iniquity in the Hebrew is *evel* or *avel.* It means perverseness, wickedness, *dishonesty,* wrong injustice, unrighteousness, depravity.

It was in the garden that satan had his first encounter with man and it was there that he lied to the woman about the tree of the knowledge of good and evil.

Now the serpent was more subtil than any beast of the field which the Lord God had made. And he said unto the woman, Yea, hath God said, Ye shall not eat of every tree of the garden? And the woman said unto the serpent, We may eat of the fruit of the trees of the garden: but of the fruit of the tree which is in the midst of the garden, God hath said, Ye shall not eat of it, neither shall ye touch it, lest ye die. And the serpent said unto the woman, Ye shall not surely die: for God doth know that in the day ye eat thereof, then your eyes shall be opened, and ye shall be as gods, knowing good and evil. (Genesis 3:1-5)

In the conversation in the garden between the woman and the serpent, we see that he very subtly got her to agree with him. In verse 3 she says that God said, "neither shall ye touch it!" God never said anything about touching the tree. Because the woman did not say exactly what God said, she altered the truth and it set her up for the "Big-lie." Satan knew what God had said, but realized she did not know and used it against her. He does the same thing with us if we allow him.

Jesus said in John 8:44 that satan is the father of lies.

Ye are of your father the devil, and the lusts of your father ye will do. He was a murderer from the beginning, and abode not in the truth, because there is no truth in him. When he speaketh a lie, he speaketh of his own: for he is a liar, and the father of it.

The Scriptures say that "there is no truth in him." He cannot tell the truth. "He speaketh of his own" when he speaks; it's out of the very nature of who he is: a liar! Lying usually stems from a selfish motive; People lie for something they want, something they feel, or something they're hiding to protect themselves.

When mankind fell, they took on satan's nature, the sin nature—the nature to lie and cover up. That's why, when they heard the voice of the Lord walking in the cool of the day, they hid themselves.

And they heard the voice of the Lord God walking in the garden in the cool of the day: and Adam and his wife hid themselves from the presence of the Lord God amongst the trees of the garden. (Genesis 3:8)

Adam took on that nature when he refused to accept responsibility for his actions and blamed the woman. Actually, not only did he blame the woman, but he blamed God as well.

*And the man said, The woman whom **Thou** gavest to be with me, she gave me of the tree, and I did eat.* (Genesis 3:12)

We cannot keep passing the blame. Truth is the foundation and the backbone of the Church. The Church is to be the sustaining force in the earth.

We who are throughout the Body of Christ must understand that God has called us to walk in truth. Where truth has fallen, iniquity will abound.

None calleth for justice, nor any pleadeth for truth: they trust in vanity, and speak lies; they conceive mischief, and bring forth iniquity. (Isaiah 59:4)

All of chapter 59 talks about the sin of a nation. Yet it's shocking because as we look around today, it's as if Isaiah wrote about the United States of America. Notice verses 13-16:

In transgressing and lying against the Lord, and departing away from our God, speaking oppression and revolt, conceiving and uttering from the heart words of falsehood. And judgment is turned away backward, and justice standeth afar off: for truth is fallen in the street, and equity cannot enter. Yea, truth faileth; and he that departeth from evil maketh himself a prey: and the Lord saw it, and it displeased Him that there was no judgment. And

He saw that there was no man, and wondered that there was no intercessor: therefore His arm brought salvation unto Him; and His righteousness, it sustained Him.

Verse 14 says that "truth is fallen in the street!" Where there is no truth, there is no justice. It is mercy and truth that purges iniquity.

By mercy and truth iniquity is purged: and by the fear of the Lord men depart from evil. (Proverbs 16:6)

It is the Church that is to uphold the truth that ultimately brings justice. Somewhere we dropped the banner and the Lord is telling us to pick it back up so the Body can get back on course. We are the light in the world. Truth starts with us individually and then corporately.

We can no longer make excuses or pass the blame onto someone else for the inconsistencies or failures in our lives. Most of our lives, before Christ, had been ones of compromise and reasoning. If we are going to walk in the way of truth and grow, however, then we must be willing to face the truth about ourselves, our situations, and our circumstances. We must also be willing to let the Spirit of truth do the work He was sent to do—causing us to say, "Remove from me the way of lying [dishonesty, compromise]: and grant me Thy law graciously. I have chosen the way of truth: Thy judgments have I laid before me" (Ps. 119:29-30).

Chapter Two

The Spirit
of Truth

*I have yet many things to say unto you, but ye cannot bear them now. Howbeit when He, **the Spirit of truth**, is come, He will guide you into all truth....* (John 16:12-13)

The judicial system is set up to work in a way that is supposed to be fair and just. However, what makes it work and what brings about fair results is the assumption that the information presented is true, or *truth,* by the court. When people take the witness stand they take an oath, and that oath is this: "I promise to tell the truth, the whole truth, and nothing but the truth, so help me God." I find this statement very interesting. You see, without the help of the Holy Spirit, it is not likely that a person will continually walk in the truth or even tell the truth. The key words are "Help me God!"

Jesus told the disciples in Acts 1:4 to "wait for the promise of the Father." The promise He was talking about can be found in John 14:16-17, 26.

And I will pray the Father, and He shall give you another Comforter, that He may abide with you for ever; even the Spirit of truth; whom the world cannot receive, because it seeth Him not, neither knoweth Him: but ye know Him; for He dwelleth with you, and shall be in you. ...But the Comforter, which is the Holy Ghost, whom the Father will send in My name, He shall teach you all things, and bring all things to your remembrance, whatsoever I have said unto you.

The promise was that He would send the Comforter, the Spirit of truth. Jesus went on to tell the disciples in Acts 1:8 that they would receive power after the Holy Ghost came upon them.

But ye shall receive power, after that the Holy Ghost is come upon you: and ye shall be witnesses unto Me both in Jerusalem, and in all Judaea, and in Samaria, and unto the uttermost part of the earth.

Only with this power would they be able to withstand the persecution ahead of them. It is only after being filled with the Spirit of truth that they could walk in the way of truth, not compromising the Word, not giving in to the pressures of life, but standing firm on the foundation of God's Word.

We cannot walk in truth, the way of truth, without having resident within us the Spirit of truth. It's not enough to be filled with the Spirit; we must also be yielded to the Spirit. John 16:5-15 outlines what the Spirit of truth has come to do.

But now I go My way to Him that sent Me; and none of you asketh Me, Whither goest Thou? But because I have said these things unto you, sorrow hath filled your heart. Nevertheless I tell you the truth; It is expedient for you that I go away: for if I go not away, the Comforter will not come unto you; but if I depart, I will send Him unto you. And when He is come, He will reprove the world of sin, and of righteousness, and of judgment: of sin, because they believe not on Me: of righteousness, because I go to My Father, and ye see Me no more; of judgment, because the prince of this world is judged. I have yet many things to say unto you, but ye cannot bear them now. Howbeit when He, the Spirit of truth, is come, He will guide you into all truth: for He shall not speak of Himself; but whatsoever He shall hear, that shall He speak: and He will shew you things to come. He shall glorify Me: for He shall receive of Mine, and shall shew it unto you. All things that the Father hath are Mine: therefore said I, that He shall take of Mine, and shall shew it unto you. (John 16:5-15)

Notice that verse 13 says "He will guide you into all truth." One thing that we as believers must understand is, when the Holy Spirit starts revealing truth, He wants to start with us.

The first thing He wants to do is guide us into *all truth* concerning ourselves. I once heard someone say there are four parts to every person. First, there's the part that you see and know, that others see and know. Second, there's the part of you that others see that you don't see. Third, there's the part you know about that others don't know about. Finally, there's the part you don't know about and others don't know about, but only God knows about.

It is also the work of the Holy Spirit, the Spirit of truth, to help us address those areas of our lives that are inconsistent with the Word of God. The Spirit of truth comes shining the light of God's Word onto these dark areas of our lives so we can address the issues that He points out and make the changes in our lives.

It's as if the heart had many rooms. We are willing to let the Lord occupy the living room and kitchen, but not the bedrooms or basement. We will address issues that are comfortable for us, but many times we deny that the tougher issues are even there. To walk in the way of truth, we must allow the Spirit of truth to reveal those dark, hidden areas and allow Him to help us change. It is through His power that we are able to face the truth.

Truth oftentimes hurts, but remember that He also is the Comforter. The word for comforter in the Greek is *paraklētos*. It means "he who has been or may be called to help, a helper" (#3875 Strong's). The word we use most often is "paraclete." He is the one to come alongside you. It's like seeing the picture of a father walking with a child, his arm around that child. As they walk, the father points to different things. You can tell by their facial expressions and closeness that they are agreeing together as they walk. That's the way the Spirit of truth is to work in our lives.

There are times when the Holy Spirit shares with us something pertaining to the future, and it may not always be something pleasant. But the blessing in His telling us is knowing that He will be there with us to help us. This was Paul's situation in Acts 20.

And now, compelled by the Spirit, I am going to Jerusalem, not knowing what will happen to me there. I only know that in every city the Holy Spirit warns me that prison and hardships are facing me. However, I consider my life worth nothing to me, if only I may finish the race and complete the task the Lord Jesus has given me—the task of testifying to the gospel of God's grace. (Acts 20:22-24 NIV)

And now, you see, I am going to Jerusalem, bound by the (Holy) Spirit, and obligated and compelled by the [convictions of my own] spirit, not knowing what will befall me there—except that the Holy Spirit clearly and emphatically affirms to me in city after city that imprisonment and suffering await me. But none of these things move me; neither do I esteem my life dear to myself, if only I may finish my course

with joy, and the ministry which I have ob-
tained from [which was entrusted to me by] the
Lord Jesus, faithfully to attest to the good news
(Gospel) of God's grace (His unmerited favor,
spiritual blessing and mercy). (Acts 20:22-24
AMP)

Notice Paul said he did not know what awaited
him—except that the Holy Spirit, *the Spirit of truth,*
told him imprisonment and suffering were waiting
for him. He accepted what the Holy Spirit shared
with him even though it meant rough times ahead.
His motivation was that he might finish his course
with joy! What Paul understood was, "Even if it costs
me my life, I will at least have faithfully finished my
part in the Kingdom." This should be our response to
the Spirit of truth no matter what He shares with us.

In John 8:32 Jesus said, "And ye shall know the
truth, and the truth shall make you free." When He
says *"know the truth,"* He's saying that you are in
agreement and acknowledgment of the facts being
presented. When the Spirit of truth speaks to our
hearts concerning an area of our lives or even an at-
titude toward a brother or sister, the only way He
can do His work and you and I can be set free is for
us to get into agreement with what He is saying and
showing us.

Many times we have bitterness and unforgive-
ness in our hearts toward someone and rather than

acknowledge those feelings and ask the Lord to help us with them, we carry them around, all the while smiling in the face of the person we don't like. We even compliment people with our lips, but in our hearts we are saying something totally different. It is what's in our heart that the Lord is listening to and the Spirit of truth wants to expose. Sometimes we look at people and we think that they are arrogant and full of pride. Then the Holy Spirit, the Spirit of *truth,* comes to you or I and says, "The problem is not them! It's you! It's you because your heart is filled with envy and jealousy toward those people." We must be willing to hear the truth.

All too often when truth comes we deny what faces us. Truth usually means change on our part and most of us have difficulty changing. We would rather make excuses or pass the blame onto someone else than to accept total responsibility for our condition.

Our proper response to truth, no matter how painful it is, must be, "I see what You are showing me. I hear what You are speaking to me. Now help me make the changes in my life."

I am sure you know that when the Holy Spirit asks a question, it's not because He doesn't know the answer. He is trying to bring something to our attention—something that we need to address. In our own unique way we can keep putting Him off, but He doesn't forget and will be back to address that same issue at a later time.

Ephesians 4:30 says, "And grieve not the holy Spirit of God, whereby ye are sealed unto the day of redemption." I believe the Holy Spirit is grieved when we deny the truth that He is trying to get us to accept. It's one thing to tell a lie; it's something altogether different to live a lie!

We live a lie when we try to be something that we *know* we are not. We live out someone else's expectations of us. Many are in ministry positions today because of someone else's expectations. All the while they know that they are not being true to who they really are. This is what happens in many relationships. Even couples try to live out the expectations of each other and finally the relationship or the marriage ends in destruction because it was never founded on *truth*! I don't believe there is anyone more miserable in life than a person trapped in living out a lie rather than taking the risk to speak the truth. At some point we must be willing to say, without embarrassment or condemnation, "I can't do it!" It's these kinds of statements that cause truth to prevail. We *can* find the power and courage to do this.

Being transformed from the kingdom of darkness to the Kingdom of light is to be transformed from the kingdom of lies to the Kingdom of truth. To walk in the Kingdom of truth, it takes the Spirit of truth. It is the Spirit of truth who gives us the power and ability to speak the truth.

Somehow the Church must come back to the basics and realize that without truth as our foundation, we are no different from the world. Ephesians 4:17-32 tells us the new way to live:

This I say therefore, and testify in the Lord, that ye henceforth walk not as other Gentiles walk, in the vanity of their mind, having the understanding darkened, being alienated from the life of God through the ignorance that is in them, because of the blindness of their heart: who being past feeling have given themselves over unto lasciviousness, to work all uncleanness with greediness. But ye have not so learned Christ; if so be that ye have heard Him and have been taught by Him, as the truth is in Jesus: that ye put off concerning the former conversation the old man, which is corrupt according to the deceitful lusts; and be renewed in the spirit of your mind; And that ye put on the new man, which after God is created in righteousness and true holiness. **Wherefore putting away lying, speak every man truth with his neighbour: for we are members one of another.** *Be ye angry, and sin not: let not the sun go down upon your wrath: neither give place to the devil. Let him that stole steal no more: but rather let him labour, working with his hands the thing which is good, that he may have to give to him that needeth. Let no corrupt* *communication proceed out of your mouth, but that which is good to the use of edifying, that it may minister grace unto the hearers. And grieve not the holy Spirit of God, whereby ye are sealed unto the day of redemption. Let all bitterness, and wrath, and anger, and clamour, and evil speaking, be put away from you, with all malice: and be ye kind one to another, tenderhearted, forgiving one another, even as God for Christ's sake hath forgiven you.* (Ephesians 4:17-32)

Notice that verse 25 says, "Wherefore putting away lying, speak every man truth with his neighbour: for we are members of one another." One of the things that should separate us from the world is our dealings and relationships being based on truth.

Colossians 3:9-10 says:

Lie not one to another, seeing that ye have put off the old man with his deeds; and have put on the new man, which is renewed in knowledge after the image of Him that created him.

When someone enters the Kingdom of God, we should tell him that this Kingdom is built upon the foundation of truth. It is the Spirit of truth who helps us with this new code of ethics. Everything we do now must be based on truth.

I believe the Church, the Body of Christ, must come to an abrupt halt and say, "Wait a minute."

Let's stop playing the games of this world and begin to operate as the Church was ordained to function. You see, satan isn't concerned about the blatant lies and disregard for the truth. Satan knows that if he can keep the Church lying subtly to one another, then ultimately he will still have the same effect on the Church that he has in the world. Very slowly the Church has lost its power and influence in the earth. It has nothing to do with Jesus; His power is still the same. It has everything to do with you and me. We are the ones called out of darkness into His light. We are the ones who are to represent His Kingdom in the earth. We are the ones who must stand up at any cost and declare the truth, not truth as we see it, but the truth according to the Word of God. It starts with speaking to one another. Before we can stand for truth in the world, we must be willing to speak the truth to one another. We have the ability to do it. We have the Spirit of truth to help us. Let's start right now, today.

Chapter Three

Speaking the Truth in Love

But speaking the truth in love, may grow up into Him in all things, which is the head, even Christ: from whom the whole body fitly joined together and compacted by that which every joint supplieth, according to the effectual working in the measure of every part, maketh increase of the body unto edifying of itself in love. (Ephesians 4:15-16)

Being involved with music almost all my life has allowed me to come in contact with many people. God has been gracious toward me and some of my songs are known around the country and abroad. Every now and then someone will come to me and say he is a songwriter or that she has a song she would like me to listen to and tell her what I think of it. I am always blessed and honored that they would even ask my opinion.

On one occasion a gentleman asked me to meet with him to critique some of his songs. I said sure and set up a time for us to meet. When I met with him I asked him to play whatever he wanted me to hear. As he played I noticed that he was very nervous and had difficulty finding the chords. He sang through about two or three songs and asked me what I thought. I told him that I could tell he was nervous but that that would go away as he continued to practice. I told him that his songs needed to be more developed but there were some nice things that I heard in all of the songs he played. We concluded our meeting and much to my surprise, I found out later that he was offended by what I had said. He told his cousin, who now happens to be one of my closest friends, that I was conceited and thought I was this and that, and that all I did was put him and his music down.

Now when I thought back through our meeting I asked the Lord if anything I said was out of order. I thought about what I said and even how I said it. I only knew for sure that I told the truth. Then I realized something—he might not have been looking for the truth. He might have wanted encouragement or even my endorsement of what he was doing; however, what I gave him was the truth. The truth is not always easy to swallow, especially when it's not what we expect.

Our ability to "speak the truth in love" is an important part of our growing up in Christ. I have found that many in the Body are not telling the truth. Many are even afraid to tell the truth because they fear rejection and alienation from others in the Body. Know this! The Father is grieved that we who are to be His glorious Church are holding one another in bondage because we do not speak the truth in love.

And He gave some, apostles; and some, prophets; and some, evangelists; and some, pastors and teachers; for the perfecting of the saints, for the work of the ministry, for the edifying of the body of Christ: till we all come in the unity of the faith, and of the knowledge of the Son of God, unto a perfect man, unto the measure of the stature of the fulness of Christ: that we henceforth be no more children, tossed to and fro, and carried about with every wind of doctrine, by the sleight of men, and cunning craftiness, whereby they lie in wait to deceive; but speaking the truth in love, may grow up into Him in all things, which is the head, even Christ: from whom the whole body fitly joined together and compacted by that which every joint supplieth, according to the effectual working in the measure of every part, maketh increase of the body unto the edifying of itself in love. (Ephesians 4:11-16)

Notice that verses 11 and 12 mention the five-fold ministry gifts the Lord placed in the Body for the perfecting or maturing of the saints. The Scriptures go on to state that we should be "no more children, tossed to and fro, and carried about with every wind of doctrine." But verse 15 says that we, "speaking the truth in love, may grow up into Him." Then we read in verse 16 that we all have a part in the maturing process.

The Church is not maturing because we have stopped speaking the truth in love. Now you need to understand what "in love" means. The word *love* there comes from the Greek word *agapē*. This is the

God-kind of love. In the King James Version it is translated as "charity," meaning benevolent love. "Its benevolence, however, is not shown by doing what the person loved desires, but what the one who loves deems as needed by the one loved" (#26 Strong's). That's what speaking the truth in love means. It's not saying what people want to hear, but telling them what they need to hear.

We have many people in the Body, some even in five-fold ministry offices, who are out of place because no one would tell them the truth in love. There are those who are calling themselves pastors when they are really evangelists. Thus the congregation gets fiery messages but never the shepherding or teaching that causes them to grow and mature. In some denominations when someone feels called to ministry, they think it means a preaching ministry, but that's just not true. We are doing more harm than good in letting someone believe one thing, when we know and can see differently. What we do to keep from hurting the person's feelings is not tell them the truth; but this is wrong. We should tell them what we really think.

I believe that with the re-establishment of the offices of the prophet and the apostle, truth will once again be spoken more consistently, thus re-establishing the foundation of truth the Church is built upon.

God has always used the prophets and apostles to speak truth and set things in order. It was a prophet who came to Eli about his sons.

And there came a man of God unto Eli, and said unto him, Thus saith the Lord, Did I plainly appear unto the house of thy father, when they were in Egypt in Pharaoh's house? And did I choose him out of all the tribes of Israel to be My priest, to offer upon Mine altar, to burn incense, to wear an ephod before Me? and did I give unto the house of thy father of the offerings made by fire of the children of Israel? Wherefore kick ye at My sacrifice and at Mine offering, which I have commanded in My habitation; and honourest thy sons above Me, to make yourselves fat with the chiefest of all the offerings of Israel My people? Wherefore the Lord God of Israel saith, I said indeed that thy house, and the house of thy father, should walk before Me for ever: but now the Lord saith, Be it far from Me; for them that honour Me I will honour, and they that despise Me shall be lightly esteemed. Behold, the days come, that I will cut off thine arm, and the arm of thy father's house, that there shall not be an old man in thine house. And thou shalt see an enemy in My habitation, in all the wealth which God shall give Israel: and there shall not be an old man in thine house for ever. And the man of thine, whom I shall not cut off from Mine altar, shall be to consume thine eyes, and to grieve thine heart: and all the increase of thine house shall die in the flower of their age. And this shall be a sign unto thee, that shall come upon thy two sons, on Hophni and Phinehas; in one day they shall die both of them. (1 Samuel 2:27-34)

It was the prophet Samuel whom God sent to Saul when Saul disobeyed Him.

Then came the word of the Lord unto Samuel, saying, It repenteth Me that I have set up Saul to be king: for he is turned back from following Me, and hath not performed My commandments. And it grieved Samuel; and he cried unto the Lord all night. And when Samuel rose early to meet Saul in the morning, it was told Samuel, saying, Saul came to Carmel, and, behold, he set him up a place, and is gone about, and passed on, and gone down to Gilgal. And Samuel came to Saul: and Saul said unto him, Blessed be thou of the Lord: I have performed the commandment of the Lord. And Samuel said, What meaneth then this bleating of the sheep in mine ears, and the lowing of the oxen which I hear? And Saul said, They have brought them from the Amalekites: for the people spared the best of the sheep and of the oxen, to sacrifice unto the Lord thy God; and the rest we have utterly destroyed. Then Samuel said unto Saul, Stay, and I will tell thee what the Lord hath said to me this night. And he said unto him, Say on. And Samuel said, When thou wast little in thine own sight, wast thou not made the head of the tribes of Israel, and the Lord anointed thee king over Israel? And the Lord sent thee on a journey, and said, Go and utterly destroy the sinners the Amalekites, and fight against them until they be consumed. Wherefore then didst thou not obey the voice of the Lord, but didst fly upon the spoil, and didst evil in the sight of the Lord? And Saul said unto Samuel, Yea, I have obeyed the voice of the Lord, and have gone the way which the Lord sent me, and have brought Agag the king of Amalek, and have utterly destroyed the Amalekites. But the people took of the spoil, sheep and oxen, the chief of the things which should have been utterly destroyed, to sacrifice unto the Lord thy God in Gilgal. And Samuel said, Hath the Lord as great delight in burnt offerings and sacrifices, as in obeying the voice of the Lord? Behold, to obey is better than sacrifice, and to hearken than the fat of rams. For rebellion is as the sin of witchcraft, and stubbornness is as iniquity and idolatry. Because thou hast rejected the word of the Lord, He hath also rejected thee from being king. (1 Samuel 15:10-23)

It was the prophet Nathan whom God sent to King David after David had committed adultery and murder.

And the Lord sent Nathan unto David. And he came unto him, and said unto him, There were two men in one city; the one rich, and the other poor. The rich man had exceeding many flocks and herds: But the poor man had nothing, save one little ewe lamb, which he had bought and nourished up: and it grew up together with him, and with his children; it did eat of his own meat, and drank of his own cup, and lay in his bosom, and was unto him as a daughter. And there came a traveller unto the rich man, and he spared to take of his own flock and of his own herd, to dress for the wayfaring man that was come unto him; but took the poor man's lamb, and dressed it for the man that was come to him. And David's anger was greatly kindled against the man; and he said to Nathan, As the Lord liveth, the man that hath done this thing shall surely die: And he shall restore the lamb fourfold, because he did this thing, and because he had no pity. And Nathan said to David, Thou art the man. Thus saith the Lord God of Israel, I anointed thee king over Israel, and I delivered thee out of the hand of Saul; And I gave thee thy master's house, and thy master's wives into thy bosom, and gave thee the house of Israel and of Judah; and if that had been too little, I would moreover have given unto thee such and such things. Wherefore hast thou despised the commandment of the Lord, to do evil in His sight? thou hast killed Uriah the Hittite with the sword, and hast taken his wife to be thy wife, and hast slain him with the sword of the children of Ammon. (2 Samuel 12:1-9)

The examples could go on, but I believe you can see the pattern here.

In Paul's letters we see him in the office of an apostle. In most cases he is setting things in order and in every case he's speaking the truth even at the expense of friendships.

It's time for those who see with the eyes of God to speak the truth. It may mean saying to someone, "You're out of place" or "This is not where your anointing is." I've seen too many situations where a person was operating outside of his gifting and anointing, and no one would address it. That kind of thing is coming to an end. Through the apostles and the prophets, God will set things in order. These offices are not popular and often times are misunderstood, but these are the ones who are not afraid to speak the truth even if it costs them their lives. As you can see in the Scriptures, it often did.

Proverbs 27:6 says this:

Faithful are the wounds of a friend; but the kisses of an enemy are deceitful.

"Faithful are the wounds of a friend." A true friend will not tell you what you want to hear, but what you need to hear. As the Body of Christ, we should endeavor to walk in truth more than any other people on the face of the earth. Often what stops us is the fear of rejection. Not only do we become fearful to share the truth about ourselves, but we hold back from speaking the truth to others about themselves. Now I know truth is not the most comfortable place in which to stand. The apostle Paul even talks about it in Galatians 4:16: "Am I therefore become your enemy, because I tell you the truth?" It's hard to speak the truth sometimes; however, it's the safest place for you and I.

When we look in the Scriptures we can find that truth was always met with opposition.

> *Jesus said unto them, Verily, verily, I say unto you, Before Abraham was, I am. Then took they up stones to cast at Him: but Jesus hid Himself, and went out of the temple, going through the midst of them, and so passed by.* (John 8:58-59)

You can see that these people's response to the truth was an attempt to kill Jesus. In Acts 7:54-60 Stephen was stoned for speaking the truth.

> *When they heard these things, they were cut to the heart, and they gnashed on him with their teeth. But he, being full of the Holy Ghost,*

looked up stedfastly into heaven, and saw the glory of God, and Jesus standing on the right hand of God, and said, Behold, I see the heavens opened, and the Son of man standing on the right hand of God. Then they cried out with a loud voice, and stopped their ears, and ran upon him with one accord, and cast him out of the city, and stoned him: and the witnesses laid down their clothes at a young man's feet, whose name was Saul. And they stoned Stephen, calling upon God, and saying, Lord Jesus, receive my spirit. And he kneeled down, and cried with a loud voice, Lord, lay not this sin to their charge. And when he had said this, he fell asleep. (Acts 7:54-60)

What happens all too often is this. When someone comes and is speaking truth into our lives and it's something we don't want to deal with, we *kill* the relationship. You see that they killed Stephen because of the truth; they killed the apostles because of the truth; they killed Jesus because of the truth. That's exactly what you and I do to people who speak truth. We distance ourselves from those people and say that the Lord is doing something different in our lives when the truth is, we are running.

Many people run from one church to another because they are running from the truth. As long as the messages are shallow and very superficial they stay, but as soon as God begins to reveal truth, these people are much like the ones in John 6. Those became offended by the truth Jesus was teaching. Notice what the Scriptures say:

Many therefore of His disciples, when they had heard this, said, This is an hard saying; who can hear it? When Jesus knew in Himself that His disciples murmured at it, He said unto them, Doth this offend you? What and if ye shall see the Son of man ascend up where He was before? It is the spirit that quickeneth; the flesh profiteth nothing: the words that I speak unto you, they are spirit, and they are life. But there are some of you that believe not. For Jesus knew from the beginning who they were that believed not, and who should betray Him. And He said, Therefore said I unto you, that no man can come unto Me, except it were given unto him of My Father. From that time many of His disciples went back, and walked no more with Him. (John 6:60-66)

It says that many "walked no more with Him!" They turned back! It was all because He began to speak truth. This is where some church members begin to talk against the pastor and the leadership because that word of truth hits them right where they live. Rather than accept the truth and be set free, we tend to run some place else, to some other church where we feel more comfortable.

We make ourselves less available for phone calls or conversation and then wonder why we are so lonely. It's at this point in our walk that we can become judgmental toward others. We are trying so hard not to deal with the realities in our own lives that we are continually pointing out everyone else's failures and shortcomings. This is a very dangerous place to be in. Proverbs 27:17 says this: "Iron sharpeneth iron; so a *man sharpeneth the countenance of his friend.*" That means we are going to have to rub up against one another. It's not always going to feel good. Sometimes we are not going to like it at all, but in the end we will be better for it.

I had a friend I grew up with. We were very close. As we became adults, we grew apart. One day he called me and asked my opinion on something he was about to do. I told him that all I could share was what the Bible said on the matter. He told me that sometimes we have to stray from the Bible. From that conversation on, our relationship has never been the same. There was a time when I would have told him what he wanted to hear, but I knew I would not be true to myself or to God unless I told him *the truth in love!*

I have found that true friends stick with each other. The more the relationship is built on truth, the stronger it becomes and it will usually stand the test of time. True friendship means commitment no matter what is revealed. Unfortunately in the Body of Christ many are afraid to share the truth about themselves or their situation. For that reason, many are walking around hurting and in need of ministry.

Someone needs to stand up and say, "It's okay to say I hurt sometimes. It's okay to say I blew it; it's okay to say I need help." God never intended for us to be super Christians. In fact, He knew that wasn't possible. That's why He sent the Holy Spirit—to strengthen us and guide us. The enemy has spread this false doctrine of speaking only positive statements, never what the current situation is. That leads people to false hopes and being deceived.

There is nothing wrong with confessing who you are in Christ. As a matter of fact, I encourage it because as we familiarize ourselves with what God's Word has to say about us, it makes the Holy Spirit's job easier in showing us where we are living up to God's Word and where we are being inconsistent. What we must be careful of, though, is deception.

Deception is when you or I take something that is close to the truth and call it truth, even though we know deep inside that it is not the truth. Many brothers and sisters are walking around with spiritual masks on that say "Praise the Lord!"..."I'm the head, not the tail!"..."I'm more than a conqueror"..."I'm blessed going in, I'm blessed going out." All the while on the inside they are miserable, confused, and hurting. The only way to receive the help needed is to say, "*Help!*"

God can move only in the truth. That's the realm and domain that He operates in.

For the word of the Lord is right; and all His works are done in truth. (Psalm 33:4)

The Lord is nigh unto all them that call upon Him, to all that call upon Him in truth. (Psalm 145:18)

My wife and I have a friend who, before giving her life to the Lord, was involved in drug trafficking. She is now a precious sister in the Lord. However, sometime after her conversion she was arrested for those dealings. Through the counsel of some well-meaning saints she was told her past was under the blood so there was no need to admit her guilt. So she pleaded not guilty. As the trial went on, everyone else involved pleaded guilty and bargained for lesser sentences. This friend, however, would not plea bargain and maintained her innocence, believing that it was in her past and under the blood of Jesus. There was one major problem. She was guilty of the charges, but would not admit the truth. God can work only with truth.

When the day of her sentencing came, all those who pled guilty received reduced sentences, but the young lady who pled not guilty received the longest sentence. Many were upset and wondered how this could be. She is a Christian, committed to the Lord now. What went wrong? She never admitted the truth! First John 1:9 says, "If we *confess our sins, He is faithful and just to forgive us our sins and to cleanse us from all unrighteousness.*"

The word *confess* here comes from the Greek word *homologeō*. It means to "speak agreeable to fact and truth" (#3670 Strong's). I believe with all my heart that this sister's sentence would have been much less if she had simply told the truth.

I need to share a personal experience that happened in my life. Some years ago I used to work for a child care agency. I worked in a cottage with anywhere from 5 to 15 boys. There were a number of Christians who worked in this cottage. One was my supervisor. Her boss and another co-worker were also Christians.

One day while working in the cottage with this co-worker, we had to discipline some of the boys for negative behavior. The following day the boys went to school and relayed to the teachers that they had been disciplined harshly. Now, any time a complaint or accusation is made against an employee in this field of work, the agency always investigates the circumstances. This also means that the employees are investigated.

Upon arriving to work that evening, I was told that I was being investigated along with my co-worker. I was told that I could have union representation if I wanted it or I could tell them what happened. Immediately I denied that anything had happened and that I would not discuss it without a union representative. My co-worker had already taken the same stand.

The problem was, he and I both knew we had overstepped our authority in the way we disciplined the boys. We both knew that we were lying. After meeting with union representatives, I felt even worse. Their counsel was, "If they can't prove it, it didn't happen." For the next day, I was miserable as the Spirit of God dealt with my heart. I could not pray because I knew I was wrong. All the staff knew that we were Christians and we had even ministered to the boys on the grounds.

Finally, I called my supervisor and told her I needed to talk with her. She called her boss and I met with the two of them. I told them my earlier statements were not true and that what was most important to me was my walking uprightly before God. I told them that I was a man of God and must tell the truth. After telling them exactly what happened, they thanked me for my honesty and assured me that they would speak on my behalf in the investigation report. They said they were shocked by my honesty because they could not prove anything. Upon my confession the other brother came forth with some reluctance and told the truth as well.

He and I both received minimal consequences for our actions and went on to work for a long time in that cottage. We even went back and apologized to the boys and to this very day I have very good relationships with the lady who was my supervisor and the gentleman who was hers.

It's when we tell the truth, speak the truth, that the Lord can move on our behalf. When we start speaking openly with one another, we can say to a brother or sister, "I love you, but I need to let you know that my feelings were hurt when you..." or, "Brother, I praise God for your zeal, but this is not the right time for you to go forth in ministry..." When we simply allow someone to speak honestly to us without judging them, then we will truly see the fruit and maturity that comes from *speaking the truth in love.*

Chapter Four

The Word Is Truth

Sanctify them through Thy truth: Thy word is truth. (John 17:17)

In John 17 Jesus made it clear that the Word is truth. He prayed to the Father and said, "Sanctify them." That word for sanctify comes from the Greek word *hagiazō*. One of its meanings is to "withdraw from fellowship with the world and from selfishness by first gaining fellowship with God" (#31 Strong's). You cannot walk in "the way of truth" and be in fellowship with the world. Truth always brings light and revelation. The Word says, "Thy Word is a *lamp* unto my feet and a *light* unto my path" (Ps. 119:105). If the Word gives light and the Word is truth, then truth gives light.

O send out Thy light and Thy truth: let them lead me; let them bring me unto Thy holy hill, and to Thy tabernacles. (Psalm 43:3)

That's why, as born-again believers, it's important for the Word of God to be a part of our daily diet. It is by our minds and hearts being continually fed the Word that we can walk in truth. In fact, God told Joshua to meditate on it day and night.

This book of the law shall not depart out of thy mouth; but thou shalt meditate therein day and night, that thou mayest observe to do according to all that is written therein: for then thou shalt make thy way prosperous, and then thou shalt have good success. (Joshua 1:8)

Our ability to successfully walk this way is based on keeping the Word of truth. John 1:14 says:

And the Word was made flesh, and dwelt among us, (and we beheld His glory, the glory as of the only begotten of the Father,) full of grace and truth.

We know that Jesus is the Word that was made flesh. We also know that Jesus is truth. He said in John 14:6, "I am the way, the truth, and the life...." Now with that understanding, realize that every time you and I reject the truth, we are rejecting the Lord. It is the Holy Spirit, also called the Spirit of truth, who is to lead and guide us into all truth. When we reject the Word we reject truth. Jesus, the Word, and the truth are the same.

To continually resist the truth produces hardness of heart. Hebrews chapters 3 and 4 mention those who did not enter into rest because of unbelief. They refused to accept the truth! It mentions twice, in Hebrews 3:7-12 and in Hebrews 4:6-7, to "harden not your hearts."

Wherefore (as the Holy Ghost saith, To day if ye will hear His voice, harden not your hearts, as in the provocation, in the day of temptation in the wilderness: when your fathers tempted Me, proved Me, and saw My works forty years. Wherefore I was grieved with that generation, and said, They do alway err in their heart; and they have not known My ways. So I sware in My wrath, They shall not enter into My rest.) Take heed, brethren, lest there be in any of you an evil heart of unbelief, in departing from the living God. (Hebrews 3:7-12)

Seeing therefore it remaineth that some must enter therein, and they to whom it was first preached entered not in because of unbelief: again, He limiteth a certain day, saying in David, To day, after so long a time; as it is said, To day if ye will hear His voice, harden not your hearts. (Hebrews 4:6-7)

The children of Israel did not enter into rest because they did not believe God! They did not believe the truth. I have found that when I am not totally truthful, there is an unsettling feeling in my spirit. There's an unrest on the inside until I have made whatever changes necessary to come back to a place of truth. Only in truth is there rest.

In Numbers 13:1-3 God told Moses to send out spies to search to land.

And the Lord spake unto Moses, saying, Send thou men, that they may search the land of Canaan, which I give unto the children of Israel:

of every tribe of their fathers shall ye send a man, every one a ruler among them. And Moses by the commandment of the Lord sent them from the wilderness of Paran: all those men were heads of the children of Israel. (Numbers 13:1-3)

I believe one of the things that caused the spies to be divided in their report was the way Moses presented the plan. Notice what he said:

And Moses sent them to spy out the land of Canaan, and said unto them, Get you up this way southward, and go up into the mountain: and see the land, what it is; and the people that dwelleth therein, whether they be strong or weak, few or many; and what the land is that they dwell in, whether it be good or bad; and what cities they be that they dwell in, whether in tents, or in strongholds; and what the land is, whether it be fat or lean, whether there be wood therein, or not. And be ye of good courage, and bring of the fruit of the land.... (Numbers 13:17-20)

This plan gave each man the right to come back with *his own* opinion, not God's view! God said nothing about the people; He said to search the *land*. So when the spies returned, the report they gave was mixed with fear, doubt, and unbelief.

And they went and came to Moses, and to Aaron, and to all the congregation of the children of Israel, unto the wilderness of Paran, to Kadesh; and brought back word unto them, and unto all the congregation, and shewed them the fruit of the land. And they told him, and said, We came unto the land whither thou sentest us, and surely it floweth with milk and honey; and this is the fruit of it. Nevertheless the people be strong that dwell in the land, and the cities are walled, and very great: and moreover we saw the children of Anak there. The Amalekites dwell in the land of the south: and the Hittites, and the Jebusites, and the Amorites, dwell in the mountains: and the Canaanites dwell by the sea, and by the coast of Jordan. And Caleb stilled the people before Moses, and said, Let us go up at once, and possess it; for we are well able to overcome it. But the men that went up with him said, We be not able to go up against the people; for they are stronger than we. And they brought up an evil report of the land which they had searched unto the children of Israel, saying, The land, through which we have gone to search it, is a land that eateth up the inhabitants thereof; and all the people that we saw in it are men of a great stature. And there we saw the giants, the sons of Anak, which come of the giants: and

*we were in our own sight as grasshoppers, and
so we were in their sight.* (Numbers 13:26-33)

Notice that they said the land was great! However, the people were strong also. The Israelites then
began to doubt God's ability to deliver the people
into their hands. Caleb tried to calm the people down
and get them to realize that God had already promised them victory, but once again the men said, "We
be not able to go up against the people; for they are
stronger than we."

Finally, because of their fear they lied and said
that the land "eateth up the inhabitants thereof."
Their unbelief led them to reject the truth. Their
rejection of God's Word caused them to not enter into
rest.

In Numbers 14:1-10 we see that the people responded by murmuring and complaining against
Moses and Aaron.

*And all the congregation lifted up their voice,
and cried; and the people wept that night. And
all the children of Israel murmured against
Moses and against Aaron: and the whole congregation said unto them, Would God that we
had died in the land of Egypt! or would God we
had died in this wilderness! And wherefore
hath the Lord brought us into this land, to fall
by the sword, that our wives and our children*

should be a prey? were it not better for us to return into Egypt? And they said one to another, Let us make a captain, and let us return into Egypt. Then Moses and Aaron fell on their faces before all the assembly of the congregation of the children of Israel. And Joshua the son of Nun, and Caleb the son of Jephunneh, which were of them that searched the land, rent their clothes: and they spake unto all the company of the children of Israel, saying, The land, which we passed through to search it, is an exceeding good land. If the Lord delight in us, then He will bring us into this land, and give it us; a land which floweth with milk and honey. Only rebel not ye against the Lord, neither fear ye the people of the land; for they are bread for us: their defence is departed from them, and the Lord is with us: fear them not. But all the congregation bade stone them with stones. And the glory of the Lord appeared in the tabernacle of the congregation before all the children of Israel. (Numbers 14:1-10)

Rather than believe God and believe that His Word is truth, they wanted to appoint another leader and return to Egypt. They wanted to return to bondage and captivity. That's exactly what happens when we reject the Word of truth. We are saying we would rather remain in bondage than be set free.

God's punishment was severe because they did not hearken to His voice.

And the Lord said, I have pardoned according to thy word: but as truly as I live, all the earth shall be filled with the glory of the Lord. Because all those men which have seen My glory, and My miracles, which I did in Egypt and in the wilderness, and have tempted Me now these ten times, and have not hearkened to My voice; surely they shall not see the land which I sware unto their fathers, neither shall any of them that provoked Me see it: but my servant Caleb, because he had another spirit with him, and hath followed Me fully, him will I bring into the land whereinto he went; and his seed shall possess it. (Now the Amalekites and the Canaanites dwelt in the valley.) Tomorrow turn you, and get you into the wilderness by the way of the Red sea. And the Lord spake unto Moses and unto Aaron, saying, How long shall I bear with this evil congregation, which murmur against Me? I have heard the murmurings of the children of Israel, which they murmur against Me. Say unto them, As truly as I live, saith the Lord, as ye have spoken in Mine ears, so will I do to you: your carcases shall fall in this wilderness; and all that were numbered of you, according to your whole number, from twenty years old and upward, which have murmured against Me, doubtless ye shall not come into the land, concerning which I sware to make you dwell therein, save Caleb the son of Jephunneh, and Joshua the son of Nun. But your little ones, which ye said should be a prey, them will I bring in, and they shall know the land which ye have despised. But as for you, your carcases, they shall fall in this wilderness. And your children shall wander in the wilderness forty years, and bear your whoredoms, until your carcases be wasted in the wilderness. After the number of the days in which ye searched the land, even forty days, each day for a year, shall ye bear your iniquities, even forty years, and ye shall know My breach of promise. I the Lord have said, I will surely do it unto all this evil congregation, that are gathered together against Me: in this wilderness they shall be consumed, and there they shall die. (Numbers 14:20-35)

It's worth putting that passage in print here because God now speaks to us through the voice of the Holy Spirit, and He is the Spirit of truth. We must not do as the children of Israel did and reject Him. The result could be devastating.

Every time we are confronted with truth and reject it, our heart becomes more callous and begins to harden toward that issue. In John chapter 8 we see how Jesus responded to those who rejected the truth. There is an extremely important principle there for us to learn.

I have included the entire conversation between Jesus and many of the Jews who believed on Him. It starts at verse 31 and goes through verse 59. I have highlighted each of their responses to the Lord. It's important that you read through this passage before I explain this principle about truth.

Then said Jesus to those Jews which believed on Him, If ye continue in My word, then are ye My disciples indeed; and ye shall know the truth, and the truth shall make you free. **They answered Him, We be Abraham's seed, and were never in bondage to any man: how sayest Thou, Ye shall be made free?** *Jesus answered them, Verily, verily, I say unto you, Whosoever committeth sin is the servant of sin. And the servant abideth not in the house for ever: but the Son abideth ever. If the Son therefore shall make you free, ye shall be free indeed. I know that ye are Abraham's seed; but ye seek to kill Me, because My word hath no place in you. I speak that which I have seen with My Father: and ye do that which ye have seen with your father.* **They answered and said unto Him, Abraham is our father.** *Jesus saith* *unto them, If ye were Abraham's children, ye would do the works of Abraham. But now ye seek to kill Me, a man that hath told you the truth, which I have heard of God: this did not Abraham. Ye do the deeds of your father.* **Then said they to Him, We be not born of fornication; we have one Father, even God.** *Jesus said unto them, If God were your Father, ye would love Me: for I proceeded forth and came from God; neither came I of Myself, but He sent Me. Why do ye not understand My speech? even because ye cannot hear My word. Ye are of your father the devil, and the lusts of your father ye will do. He was a murderer from the beginning, and abode not in the truth, because there is no truth in him. When he speaketh a lie, he speaketh of his own: for he is a liar, and the father of it. And because I tell you the truth, ye believe Me not. Which of you convinceth Me of sin? And if I say the truth, why do ye not believe Me? He that is of God heareth God's words: ye therefore hear them not, because ye are not of God.* **Then answered the Jews, and said unto Him, Say we not well that Thou art a Samaritan, and hast a devil?** *Jesus answered, I have not a devil; but I honour My Father, and ye do dishonour Me. And I seek not Mine own glory: there is one that seeketh and judgeth. Verily, verily, I say* *unto you, If a man keep My saying, he shall never see death.* **Then said the Jews unto Him, Now we know that Thou hast a devil. Abraham is dead, and the prophets; and Thou sayest, If a man keep My saying, he shall never taste of death. Art Thou greater than our father Abraham, which is dead? and the prophets are dead: whom makest Thou Thyself?** *Jesus answered, If I honour Myself, My honour is nothing: it is My Father that honoureth Me; of whom ye say, that He is your God: yet ye have not known Him; but I know Him: and if I should say, I know Him not, I shall be a liar like unto you: but I know Him, and keep His saying. Your father Abraham rejoiced to see My day: and he saw it, and was glad.* **Then said the Jews unto Him, Thou art not yet fifty years old, and hast Thou seen Abraham?** *Jesus said unto them, Verily, verily, I say unto you, Before Abraham was, I am.* **Then took they up stones to cast at Him:** *but Jesus hid Himself, and went out of the temple, going through the midst of them, and so passed by.* (John 8:31-59)

Now that you have read this passage, I want you to first notice *that they were believers*. We find that in verse 31. In verse 32, Jesus made a statement of truth that confounded them—and the confrontation began. He said, "And ye shall know the truth, and the truth shall make you free." Immediately they rejected what He was saying! They said, *"We be Abraham's seed, and were never in bondage." They had missed the whole point of what Jesus was saying.*

Before you and I can be made free, we must first *know* the *truth*! The Lord has shown me that to know the truth is to acknowledge that what the Holy Spirit is showing us is real. To *know* the truth is to accept and agree with the Holy Spirit, the Spirit of truth. When you accepted Jesus as Savior, you did so by acknowledging the truth. The truth is that "all have sinned and come short of the glory of God" (Rom. 3:23). Once we came into agreement with that truth, we can receive the freedom that comes from accepting into our hearts He who is truth—Jesus! We not only hear the truth, but believe it.

In whom ye also trusted, after that ye heard the word of truth, the gospel of your salvation: in whom also after that ye believed, ye were sealed with that holy Spirit of promise. (Ephesians 1:13)

Because these believers were not willing to hear the truth about themselves, the conversation became more confrontational. By the time we get to verses 40-41, Jesus was speaking more directly to the nature that formed their speech. He told them that they wanted to kill Him, the Man who told them the truth. He went on to make it even more clear by saying, "Ye do the deeds of your father."

Every time He spoke truth, they made a rebuttal that was a personal attack on His character. We do this same thing when someone shares truth with us that we don't want to hear. We attack the person who is talking to us. We say, "Who do you think you are to tell me?" Or we say to someone else, "Can you believe what brother or sister so-and-so had the nerve to say to me?" We try to disqualify the person from having the right to speak in our lives. As you see in this passage of Scripture, it only makes things worse, for finally by verses 44-45, He came out and told them:

> *Ye are of your father the devil, and the lusts of your father ye will do. He was a murderer from the beginning, and abode not in the truth, because there is no truth in him. When he speaketh a lie, he speaketh of his own: for he is a liar, and the father of it. And because I tell you the truth, ye believe Me not.*

They could not hear the truth because they were not born again. Ultimately they tried to stone Him! You see, this is how truth works. The more you and I reject it, the harder it hits when it comes back. Every time they rejected what Jesus was saying, He came back with a progressively harder truth until finally He exposed them publicly for who they really were. I call it the principle of *"Operation or Demolition."*

Chapter Five

Operation or Demolition

For the word of God is quick, and powerful, and sharper than any twoedged sword, piecing even to the dividing asunder of soul and spirit, and of the joints and marrow, and is a discerner of the thoughts and intents of the heart. (Hebrews 4:12)

Is not My word like as a fire? saith the Lord; and like a hammer that breaketh the rock in pieces? (Jeremiah 23:29)

In Chapter Two we looked at the Spirit of truth and how He is to operate in our lives as the Spirit of truth. Many in the Church today think of power when they think of the Holy Spirit, and that's good. He does give us the power to live a victorious Christian life. In Acts 1:8 Jesus said, "But ye shall receive power, after that the Holy Ghost is come upon you...." We must also understand that the Holy Spirit has the responsibility to guide us into all truth. Jesus said in John 14:17, "Even the Spirit of truth; whom the world cannot receive, because it seeth Him not, neither knoweth Him: but ye know Him; for He dwelleth with you, and shall be in you."

He goes on to say in verse 26, "But the Comforter, which is the Holy Ghost, whom the Father will send in My name, He shall teach you all things, and bring all things to your remembrance, whatsoever I have said unto you."

Then in John 16:13 He said this:

Howbeit when He, the Spirit of truth, is come, He will guide you into all truth: for He shall not speak of Himself; but whatsoever He shall hear, that shall He speak: and He will shew you things to come.

So yes, the Holy Spirit brings power to our walk, but He also brings light to our hearts and lives. You see, it is the Word of God that brings about change in our lives. It is the Holy Spirit who confirms where that Word applies in our lives. So not only do we need power to stand in the midst of adversity, we also need power to change as the Word of God and the Holy Spirit directs.

As I mentioned earlier, one of the main areas we must address is the truth about ourselves. What we must realize, however, is the importance of timing. When the truth is being pointed out to us, by the Word or by the Spirit of truth, it is at that very moment that all of Heaven is ready to back us up, to follow through, once we come into agreement with that truth. Often God is wanting to address a certain issue in our lives in order to set us free and bring us into the place He desires for us. Unfortunately, you and I think we have the option or right to tell God to wait or that we'll address it at a later time. This is an assumption on our part that God's grace will continue to rest on that area until we are ready to deal with it.

This was the mistake the children of Israel made in Numbers 13 and 14. Instead of following God's directions, they became fearful and chose not to believe the truth. The truth was that God *had* given them the land and those that inhabited it. But the

Israelites had to move right then. After they rejected the report of Joshua and Caleb, they still tried to enter the Promised Land—only to be defeated. The key is this: God has a timetable He is working from and you and I need to be sensitive to His schedule. Philippians 1:6 says this:

Being confident of this very thing, that He which hath begun a good work in you will perform it until the day of Jesus Christ.

That means there is a progressive work going on in our lives that He *will* bring to completion.

It is extremely important that you understand how great God's love is for you and that once you yield your heart to Him, He will do whatever it takes to bring your life to a place of maturity and completion in Him.

It is for that reason I want to share with you this principle and process. We have already established that the Word is truth; we see that in John 17:17. When truth, or the Word, comes to you and I, it will always produce some type of change. That change will be positive or negative. You and I make that decision. In Hebrews 4:12 the Scriptures say this:

For the word of God is quick, and powerful, and sharper than any twoedged sword, piercing even to the dividing asunder of soul and spirit, and of the joints and marrow, and is a discerner of the thoughts and intents of the heart.

It says the Word is "sharper than any twoedged sword" and "is a discerner of the thoughts and intents of the heart." This is speaking of the Word, which is truth.

When truth *first* comes, it's much like a surgical *operation*. It comes in a very private way. Few if any know the details of the matter. When the matter is exposed, it's for the purpose of dealing with it and being done with it. So when truth first comes, it's like that two-edged sword ready to perform the spiritual surgery needed to bring about wholeness. However, as in natural surgery, the patient must be in agreement that there is a need for this operation and be willing to submit to the procedure. When a condition is diagnosed by a doctor, the patient has a right to what is called a "second opinion." Many of us take the same approach with the Word of God, the truth. We often try to get a second opinion from a friend, brother or sister in the Lord, or even a pastor, rather than accept the truth. When the Holy Spirit points out an area, He's not saying, "Now, if you like, you can get a second opinion." With Him there is no second opinion.

When the Holy Spirit sees that we are not willing to agree with the truth in that area, He simply leaves it alone and waits for the next opportunity to address it.

Now as I shared with you about John 8:31-59, Jesus was speaking truth and these Jews were continually rejecting it until finally they tried to kill Him.

There are certain areas in your life and mine that the Spirit of truth has had to come back more than once in order to address it. As in the example of John 8, truth comes back more forcefully each time until it becomes like a hammer. The Word in Jeremiah 23:29 says this:

Is not My word like as a fire? saith the Lord; and like a hammer that breaketh the rock in pieces?

It's also interesting to note that Jeremiah 23 is talking about *lying prophets.*

Every time we reject the truth in a certain area of our lives, that area begins to become hardened to the Word of God and to the Spirit of truth. It is God's mercy and grace that keep the truth coming to us to deal with our hearts in a more private way.

After a while, when God sees that we are not going to confess or repent, He has no other recourse than to allow truth to take more drastic measures. The Word that first came as sword has now become a hammer. What could have been accomplished by operation, now must be accomplished through demolition. Please understand that it's all the grace and mercy of God—for He is not willing to let us remain the same. It's you and I who make the choice of which process it will be.

Let me illustrate. Shortly after my wife and I were married, we needed a car. We had received an income tax refund check, so I went out looking for a good deal on a car. My brother-in-law took me to a car dealer where you "buy here, pay here." I was somewhat skeptical, but willing to look around, since my credit at the time was in no shape to finance a new car.

While looking around I came across a very clean Oldsmobile. The only problem with the car was its need of painting. The body and interior were in excellent condition. I asked the sales person if I could test drive it. It started right up and drove wonderfully. I drove it by our apartment and took my wife for a ride. She liked it too. We decided we would pray about it and if the car was still available the next day, we would buy it. The next day I went and purchased the car. It never gave us one problem.

Here's where I blew it! After about six months of payments, I went by the lot and saw this late model Lincoln Towncar. It was really sharp. I took it out for a test drive and decided that certainly the Lord had sent this car for me. Now even while I was driving it, the Holy Spirit was saying, "This is not for you," but I didn't listen. I drove it by the apartment to show it to my wife and asked her what she thought about my buying it. She said she didn't think it was the car for us. It's amazing how the Holy Spirit can sound just like your spouse! However, I was determined to have this car. So I made a deal with the salesman and in a couple of weeks I had the car. I knew in my heart that the Lord had said no, but I had to learn the hard way.

About a month after I got the car, someone broke out the back window. It took me three months to get it fixed. A month later, on Christmas morning to be exact, I went out to find all four tires slashed, the antenna broken off, and both side mirrors ripped off the car. I came to the rude awakening that *God is not obligated to keep or protect what He has not given.* This for me was an example of resisting the Spirit of truth for my own selfish desires. I finally repented and asked my wife to forgive me.

It's these kinds of personal decisions that ultimately affect the Church and ministries. I was serving in ministry at the time all of this happened. I had deceived myself into believing God wanted me to have this car. Little did I know that I was setting myself up for the hammer. We can reason with ourselves all we want to, but truth will always prevail and bring to light the reality of the situation. In truth there are no secrets.

In the 1980's we saw men in high profile ministries seemingly destroyed by secrets that were exposed in public. Many could not understand why God would allow this shame to be brought on the Church. First of all, you must recognize that *judgment begins in the house of God* (see 1 Pet. 4:17). Before God can judge the world for sin, He must first address His own children.

Secondly, it was never God's intention to see these ministries brought to shame or for the Body of Christ to have to make apologies. I happen to have been in two different meetings where the speakers for those meetings shared how they had approached two of our most prominent fallen leaders during the 1980's with specific words from the Lord. Both men denied any wrongdoing or willingness to receive counsel and help.

Their denial was rejecting the truth, and it is apparent, after the truth was revealed, that they had walked in denial for many years. What could have been a simple operation by the Word of God became a demolition site. Just as in the natural sense, when a building is being demolished it's impossible to keep that fact concealed from the public. Everyone in the general vicinity knows about it because of the explosion. There are leaders all over the Body of Christ who need to know that what God wants, more than anything else, is for His leaders to walk in truth and freedom. We have a word we say on our staff. We call it the "T-word." That word is *transparent*! We have committed to one another to be transparent. It isn't easy, but we know that it's best for our relationships and for the Body of Christ.

The love of God is so great toward you and I that He would rather expose us if necessary, than have us walk in bondage because we are not willing to acknowledge the truth. There is no way we can walk in complete freedom if we are hiding things from one another and are too proud to say, "I need help." The Body of Christ is weakened by that kind of denial. Our strength and our ability to stand is predicated on two things: that we hold one another accountable to walk in truth, and that we submit to those to whom we are accountable. What is the difference you ask? Here are some examples:

Accountability says: "I'm okay. Check me out. Everything I'm doing is okay.

Submission says: "I yield to you. I give way to you. Let me know if everything's okay. You have the 'right of way' in my life."

Accountability says: "My financial books are complete; check to see that I'm okay."

Submission says: "*You* take my financial books and keep them."

Accountability says: "My moral life is okay; look and see."

Submission says: "I submit to you; address any issues that you see or discern, or that the Holy Spirit has revealed to you concerning my moral life. I will make adjustments in the areas that you point out to me."

The leaders in the Body of Christ who failed to stand did not submit to their "accountability group" (i.e. the eldership of their denomination, Board of Directors, etc.). In the Body of Christ it is possible to have transparency and even accountability with submission. But without submission, without *the willingness to alter our life styles based on truth conveyed through those in authority*, we will never fully walk out the way of truth at a level that will produce God's best. *Transparency, accountability, and submission*—nothing else will work; nothing else will do.

If we continue to walk in a state of denial or of lying to one another, we are no better than, even no different from those under the rulership of satan. Yes, truth can sometimes be difficult to face and yet it is the most liberating feeling we can have.

You need to know that when truth comes, "mercy" is never far behind. Psalm 61:7 says:

He shall abide before God for ever: O prepare mercy and truth, which may preserve him.

In Psalm 85:10 the Word says:

Mercy and truth are met together; righteousness and peace have kissed each other.

Also, in Psalm 98:3 it says:

He hath remembered His mercy and His truth toward the house of Israel: all the ends of the earth have seen the salvation of our God.

It is God's *grace* that helps us accept the truth. Grace comes from the word *charis,* meaning "unearned or unmerited favor". *It affects man's sinfulness and not only forgives the repentant sinner, but also brings joy and thankfulness to Him* (#5485 *Hebrew-Greek Key Study Bible*). Grace helps us accept the truth as well as enables us to carry out the actions necessary to bring about the desired change. *Mercy* comes from the word *eleos,* which "concerns itself not with sin itself as does grace, but with the misery brought upon the sinner as a consequence of that sin" (#1656 Strong's).

When truth comes, it is grace that helps us accept truth. Mercy is there to help us leave behind that state of misery once truth has done the work. So once truth is accepted, and mercy and grace have done their part, then we have peace.

Peace comes from the word *eirēnē,* meaning, "absence or end of strife" (#1515 Strong's). Before there can be total peace, there must be total truth. The less we resist, the easier it is for God to accomplish His plans for our lives and His plan for the Church.

God is not in the business of airing dirty laundry, and I am certainly grateful for that. However, He is coming back for a Church that is spotless. Let's decide right now to submit to the Spirit of truth, to the work of the Word in our lives. Its inevitable truth will always prevail, praise God!

Chapter Six

The Test of Truth

Hereby ye shall be proved: By the life of Pharaoh ye shall not go forth hence, except your youngest brother come hither. Send one of you, and let him fetch your brother, and ye shall be kept in prison, that your words may be proved, whether there be any truth in you: or else by the life of Pharaoh surely ye are spies. (Genesis 42:15-16)

All of us meet with times when we are tested regarding the level of truth in which we walk. The more we know and understand about the Word of God, the more we are required to walk out. In today's times, we are faced with opportunities to compromise our walk or to stand for the truth every day. Passing the small tests then enables us to pass the big ones.

Truth stands on its own, but one lie is maintained only by another lie. Once you lie about someone or something, you usually must tell another lie to cover the first one. This is satan's way of causing you to not only be ensnared by a lie, but ultimately be held captive by the bondage that comes from not walking in truth.

Lying is habit-forming, and is motivated by a spirit of lying. That's why Psalm 119:29a says, "Remove from me the *way* of lying." It takes the power of God to break the cycle of lying.

In this chapter I want to look at the life of Joseph and how, even in the midst of the lies that were told about him and on him, he never lost sight of what God had shown him. Ultimately truth prevailed and what was hidden by his brothers was brought to light.

In Genesis chapter 37 we read about the dreams Joseph had. When sharing these dreams with his brothers, they became very envious and wanted to kill him.

And Joseph dreamed a dream, and he told it his brethren: and they hated him yet the more. And he said unto them, Hear, I pray you, this dream which I have dreamed: for, behold, we were binding sheaves in the field, and, lo, my sheaf arose, and also stood upright; and, behold, your sheaves stood round about, and made obeisance to my sheaf. And his brethren said to him, Shalt thou indeed reign over us? or shalt thou indeed have dominion over us? And they hated him yet the more for his dreams, and for his words. And he dreamed yet another dream, and told it his brethren, and said, Behold, I have dreamed a dream more; and, behold, the sun and the moon and the eleven stars made obeisance to me. And he told it to his father, and to his brethren: and his father rebuked him, and said unto him, What is this dream that thou hast dreamed? Shall I and thy mother and thy brethren indeed come to bow down ourselves to thee to the earth? (Genesis 37:5-10)

In verse 18 we see that the brothers' plan was to kill him, but Reuben came to his rescue and spoke of another plan.

And when they saw him afar off, even before he came near unto them, they conspired against him to slay him. And they said one to another, Behold, this dreamer cometh. Come now therefore, and let us slay him, and cast him into some pit, and we will say, Some evil beast hath devoured him: and we shall see what will become of his dreams. And Reuben heard it, and he delivered him out of their hands; and said, Let us not kill him. And Reuben said unto them, Shed no blood, but cast him into this pit that is in the wilderness, and lay no hand upon him; that he might rid him out of their hands, to deliver him to his father again. And it came to pass, when Joseph was come unto his brethren, that they stript Joseph out of his coat, his coat of many colours that was on him. (Genesis 37:18-23)

Later they decided to sell Joseph to the Ishmeelites.

Come, and let us sell him to the Ishmeelites, and let not our hand be upon him; for he is our brother and our flesh. And his brethren were content. Then there passed by Midianites merchantmen; and they drew and lifted up Joseph out of the pit, and sold Joseph to the Ishmeelites for twenty pieces of silver: and they brought Joseph into Egypt. (Genesis 37:27-28)

After that they took Joseph's coat, which they had dipped in blood, and gave it to their father.

And they took Joseph's coat, and killed a kid of the goats, and dipped the coat in the blood; And they sent the coat of many colours, and they brought it to their father; and said, This have we found: know now whether it be thy son's coat or no. And he knew it, and said, It is my son's coat; an evil beast hath devoured him; Joseph is without doubt rent in pieces. (Genesis 37:31-33)

Notice that they did not say he had been killed. They simply gave Jacob the coat and said they had found it. It was Jacob who said, "Joseph is without doubt rent in pieces."

Now here were the sons standing around their father knowing that Joseph was not dead. Yet none of them were willing to tell the truth. This was the beginning of many lies for them. They did not say out of their own mouths that Joseph was dead; however, they were just as guilty because they deceived their father.

Keep in mind that Joseph was 17 years old at the time. We later see that he was 30 years old when he came out of prison. That means for at least 13 years these brothers had to continue to lie and cover one another's stories about Joseph. Every time Jacob mentioned Joseph, they had to speak of him as if he were dead. They not only precipitated the lie—they had to live a lie! No doubt there were many opportunities for them to tell the truth, but none did. For at least 20 years, these men walked around imprisoned by their own lies and deceit.

In chapter 39 we see that Joseph was purchased by Potiphar and placed over the affairs of Potiphar's house.

And Joseph was brought down to Egypt; and Potiphar, an officer of Pharaoh, captain of the guard, an Egyptian, bought him of the hands of the Ishmeelites, which had brought him down thither. And the Lord was with Joseph, and he was a prosperous man; and he was in the house of his master the Egyptian. And his master saw that the Lord was with him, and that the Lord made all that he did to prosper in his hand. And Joseph found grace in his sight, and he served him: and he made him overseer over his house, and all that he had he put into his hand. And it came to pass from the time that he had made him overseer in his house, and over all that he had, that the Lord blessed the Egyptian's house for Joseph's sake; and the blessing of the Lord was upon all that he had in the house, and in the field. And he left all that he had in Joseph's hand; and he knew not ought he had, save the bread which he did eat. And Joseph was a goodly person, and well favoured. (Genesis 39:1-6)

Even in the midst of adverse conditions, God was still blessing Joseph's affairs and giving him favor with all whom he met. Joseph was an honest person, and even though it is not stated, he walked in truth. Once he had been placed over Potiphar's house, though he was tempted by Potiphar's wife.

> *And it came to pass after these things, that his master's wife cast her eyes upon Joseph; and she said, Lie with me. But he refused, and said unto his master's wife, Behold, my master wotteth not what is with me in the house, and he hath committed all that he hath to my hand; There is none greater in this house than I; neither hath he kept back any thing from me but thee, because thou art his wife: how then can I do this great wickedness, and sin against God? And it came to pass, as she spake to Joseph day by day, that he hearkened not unto her, to lie by her, or to be with her.* (Genesis 39:7-10)

It's important to note that in verse 9, Joseph's response was not one of concern about Potiphar. He was more concerned about sinning against God! He recognized that his ultimate responsibility was to God. The test here for Joseph was not whether Potiphar would find out if he had slept with his wife, but rather maintaining integrity before the Lord and walking in truth.

This is an important key for us as we walk in truth. Many times we make decisions of compromise when we feel no one will know or find out. When we walk in truth and continually acknowledge the Spirit of truth, it causes us to be sensitive to the fact that God sees and knows all things. Our decisions should be based on whether or not the thing we do is pleasing to God and will bring glory to Him. I have heard it said that a person's real character and integrity is best judged by what he does with his time when no one else is around. I think that's pretty accurate. As we can see, Joseph did not want to sin against God at any time. Unfortunately, Potiphar's wife did not stop there.

When Potiphar's wife saw that she could not get Joseph to compromise his walk, she attacked him and then lied about him once she realized his garment was left in her hand.

And it came to pass about this time, that Joseph went into the house to do his business; and there was none of the men of the house there within. And she caught him by his garment, saying, Lie with me: and he left his garment in her hand, and fled, and got him out. And it came to pass, when she saw that he had left his garment in her hand, and was fled forth, that she called unto the men of her house, and spake unto them, saying, See, he hath brought in an Hebrew unto us to mock us; he came in unto me to lie with me, and I cried with a loud voice: and it came to pass, when he heard that I lifted

*up my voice and cried, that he left his garment
with me, and fled, and got him out. And she
laid up his garment by her, until his lord came
home. And she spake unto him according to
these words, saying, The Hebrew servant, which
thou hast brought unto us, came in unto me to
mock me: And it came to pass, as I lifted up my
voice and cried, that he left his garment with
me, and fled out. And it came to pass, when his
master heard the words of his wife, which she
spake unto him, saying, After this manner did
thy servant to me; that his wrath was kindled.*
(Genesis 39:11-19)

The enemy is quick to tempt all of us. The more
we stand for truth, the more he will try to hinder
us—even to the point of creating a false situation, as
he did with Joseph.

In verse 20 we see that Joseph was put in prison
after being falsely accused, but because he was un-
willing to compromise the truth, God was still working on his behalf. We see that the same favor given to
him in Potiphar's house was given to him in prison.

*But the Lord was with Joseph, and shewed him
mercy, and gave him favour in the sight of the
keeper of the prison. And the keeper of the
prison committed to Joseph's hand all the
prisoners that were in the prison; and whatsoever they did there, he was the doer of it. The*

keeper of the prison looked not to any thing that was under his hand; because the Lord was with him, and that which he did, the Lord made it to prosper. (Genesis 39:21-23)

Romans 8:28 says this:

And we know that all things work together for good to them that love God, to them who are the called according to His purpose.

Joseph's life is a perfect example of God using all things to work for Joseph's good. It wasn't easy, and Joseph even gave to his sons names that spoke of his life.

And Joseph called the name of the firstborn Manasseh: For God, said he, hath made me forget all my toil, and all my father's house. And the name of the second called he Ephraim: For God hath caused me to be fruitful in the land of my affliction. (Genesis 41:51-52)

It is not easy to walk in truth because the one who rules the air and this world system is the father of lies: satan! That's why everything the Church does and stands for should be in total opposition to the things of this world.

In Matthew 5:10-12, Jesus said:

Blessed are they which are persecuted for righteousness' sake: for theirs is the kingdom of heaven.

Blessed are ye, when men shall revile you, and persecute you, and shall say all manner of evil against you falsely, for My sake. Rejoice, and be exceeding glad: for great is your reward in heaven: for so persecuted they the prophets which were before you.

Notice that in verse 12 He said, "so persecuted they the *prophets*"—the prophets! They're the ones who speak forth the truth.

We are able to see something else in the life of Joseph. It is that truth will always prevail! No matter how hard times are or how much opposition we might face, if we remain in truth, truth will always win. It may take a while, as in Joseph's case. As a matter of fact, if we look at his situation, it took at least 22 years for the truth to come out.

In Genesis 40 you see that Joseph met two men while in prison, a butler and a baker. They had dreams, and Joseph gave the interpretations of those dreams. The butler was returned to his position, but the baker was executed.

And it came to pass the third day, which was Pharaoh's birthday, that he made a feast unto all his servants: and he lifted up the head of the chief butler and of the chief baker among his servants. And he restored the chief butler unto his butlership again; and he gave the cup into Pharaoh's hand: But he hanged the chief baker:

as Joseph had interpreted to them. Yet did not the chief butler remember Joseph, but forgat him. (Genesis 40:20-23)

Joseph had asked that he be remembered, but as you can see, in verse 23, the butler forgot about him. Two years later the king had a dream, but no one to interpret it. That's when the butler remembered Joseph. Joseph was brought forth, explained the dream, and told Pharaoh that there would be seven plenteous years and seven years of famine.

Pharaoh knew he needed a godly man. He selected Joseph.

And the thing was good in the eyes of Pharaoh, and in the eyes of all his servants. And Pharaoh said unto his servants, Can we find such a one as this is, a man in whom the Spirit of God is? And Pharaoh said unto Joseph, Forasmuch as God hath shewed thee all this, there is none so discreet and wise as thou art: thou shalt be over my house, and according unto thy word shall all my people be ruled: only in the throne will I be greater than thou. And Pharaoh said unto Joseph, See, I have set thee over all the land of Egypt. And Pharaoh took off his ring from his hand, and put it upon Joseph's hand, and arrayed him in vestures of fine linen, and put a gold chain about his neck; and he made him to ride in the second chariot which he had; and they cried before him, Bow the knee: and he made him ruler over all the land of Egypt. And Pharaoh said unto Joseph, I am Pharaoh, and without thee shall no man lift up his hand or foot in all the land of Egypt. And Pharaoh called Joseph's name Zaphnath-paaneah; and he gave him to wife Asenath the daughter of Potipherah priest of On. And Joseph went out over all the land of Egypt. (Genesis 41:37-45)

This was the fulfillment of Joseph's dreams and the beginning of the seven years of plenty.

As we read on, we see that after the seven years of plenty, just as Joseph said, a famine came upon the land. Now everyone had to go to Egypt to get food. Genesis 42:1-3 records that Jacob sent his sons to get food.

Now when Jacob saw that there was corn in Egypt, Jacob said unto his sons, Why do ye look one upon another? And he said, Behold, I have heard that there is corn in Egypt: get you down thither, and buy for us from thence; that we may live, and not die. And Joseph's ten brethren went down to buy corn in Egypt. (Genesis 42:1-3)

They had no idea that the man Pharaoh had placed over all of Egypt was their brother. The Scriptures, however, say that Joseph knew who they were.

And Joseph saw his brethren, and he knew them, but made himself strange unto them, and spake roughly unto them; and he said unto them, Whence come ye? And they said, From the land of Canaan to buy food. And Joseph knew his brethren, but they knew not him. And Joseph remembered the dreams which he dreamed of them, and said unto them, Ye are spies; to see the nakedness of the land ye are come. And they said unto him, Nay, my lord, but to buy food are thy servants come. We are all one man's sons; we are true men, thy servants are no spies. (Genesis 42:7-11)

Once Joseph saw them, he accused them of being spies. Notice in verse 11 how they responded. They said, "We are true men." Joseph knew they were not, and in verse 13 they even lied about him.

And they said, Thy servants are twelve brethren, the sons of one man in the land of Canaan; and, behold, the youngest is this day with our father, and one is not. (Genesis 42:13)

In verse 15 Joseph told his brothers that they would be *proved!* That word also means "tested." In verse 16 he said they would be tested to see if there was any truth in them.

Hereby ye shall be proved: By the life of Pharaoh ye shall not go forth hence, except your youngest brother come hither. Send one of you, and let him fetch your brother, and ye shall be kept in prison, that your words may be proved, whether there be any truth in you: or else by the life of Pharaoh surely ye are spies. And he put them all together into ward three days. And Joseph said unto them the third day, This do, and live; for I fear God: If ye be true men, let one of your brethren be bound in the house of your prison: go ye, carry corn for the famine of your houses: But bring your youngest brother unto me; so shall your words be verified, and ye shall not die. And they did so. (Genesis 42:15-20)

The brothers knew it would be difficult for them to bring back their youngest brother, and they began to confess among themselves the wrong they had done to Joseph.

And they said one to another, We are verily guilty concerning our brother, in that we saw the anguish of his soul, when he besought us, and we would not hear; therefore is this distress come upon us. And Reuben answered them, saying, Spake I not unto you, saying, Do not sin against the child; and ye would not hear? therefore, behold, also his blood is required. (Genesis 42:21-22)

All the years of living the lie about Joseph were now coming back on them. Truth was beginning to surface and they were very uncomfortable. As you read on through chapters 43 and 44, you see that Joseph took them through a number of different tests and each one was progressively more difficult. Finally, when Joseph wanted to send them home without their youngest brother, they pleaded with him to not do that. They already had one brother who did not return to their father and if they came back without this brother, it would kill their father.

They were still trying to cover up the lie they'd started 22 years earlier. In chapter 45 it says that Joseph could not hold back any longer. (Keep in mind that this is probably two years from the time he first saw his brothers in Egypt.)

Then Joseph could not refrain himself before all them that stood by him; and he cried, Cause every man to go out from me. And there stood no man with him, while Joseph made himself known unto his brethren. and he wept aloud: and the Egyptians and the house of Pharaoh heard. And Joseph said unto his brethren, I am Joseph; doth my father yet live? And his brethren could not answer him; for they were troubled at his presence. And Joseph said unto his brethren, Come near to me, I pray you. And they came near. And he said, I am Joseph your brother, whom ye sold into Egypt. (Genesis 45:1-4)

At first they were shocked, and then fearful that the truth about what really happened to Joseph would now come out. Probably the most shocking words they'd ever heard were Joseph's proclamation: "I am Joseph your brother, whom ye sold into Egypt."

What the brothers did not understand was that Joseph was not looking for revenge. His ultimate goal was reconciliation. The brothers still returned home, though, and gave their father the news.

And they went up out of Egypt, and came into the land of Canaan unto Jacob their father. And told him, saying, Joseph is yet alive, and he is governor over all the land of Egypt. And Jacob's heart fainted, for he believed them not. And they told him all the words of Joseph, which he had said unto them: and when he saw the wagons which Joseph had sent to carry him, the spirit of Jacob their father revived: and Israel said, It is enough; Joseph my son is yet alive: I will go and see him before I die. (Genesis 45:25-28)

Joseph then brought all of his family to Egypt to live. In chapter 50 we see that after his father died, Joseph's brothers were fearful that he would do them harm. No doubt over the years since they came to Egypt Joseph had told his father exactly what happened and how he came to finally rule over the land.

We see in verses 15-18 of chapter 50 that Joseph's father asks him to forgive his brothers.

And when Joseph's brethren saw that their father was dead, they said, Joseph will peradventure hate us, and will certainly requite us all the evil which we did unto him. And they sent a messenger unto Joseph, saying, Thy father did command before he died, saying, So shall ye say unto Joseph, Forgive, I pray thee now, the trespass of thy brethren, and their sin; for they did unto thee evil: and now, we pray thee, forgive the trespass of the servants of the God of thy father. And Joseph wept when they spake unto him. And his brethren also went and fell down before his face; and they said, Behold, we be thy servants. (Genesis 50:15-18)

In the next verses you see that Joseph's heart was truly one of love and forgiveness for his brothers.

And Joseph said unto them, Fear not: for am I in the place of God? But as for you, ye thought evil against me; but God meant it unto good, to bring to pass, as it is this day, to save much people alive. Now therefore fear ye not: I will nourish you, and your little ones. And he comforted them, and spake kindly unto them. (Genesis 50:19-21)

The way of truth is often a difficult walk, but in it we have the confidence that God will make all things right. It's as we walk in truth that we are free to love and forgive. We don't have to struggle or concern ourselves with the final outcome. As truth is tested in each one of us, we can be assured that if we stand, truth will not let us down.

Chapter Seven

The Way of Truth

Remove from me the way of lying: and grant me thy law graciously. I have chosen the way of truth: thy judgments have I laid before me. (Psalm 119:29-30)

Lead me in Thy truth, and teach me: for Thou art the God of my salvation; on Thee do I wait all the day. (Psalm 25:5)

All the paths of the Lord are mercy and truth unto such as keep His covenant and His testimonies. (Psalm 25:10)

For the word of the Lord is right; and all His works are done in truth. (Psalm 33:4)

In John 18 Jesus stood before Pilate and made this statement:

Pilate therefore said unto Him, Art Thou a king then? Jesus answered, Thou sayest that I am a king. To this end was I born, and for this cause came I into the world, that I should bear witness unto the truth. Every one that is of the truth heareth My voice. (John 18:37)

Jesus came to unveil truth! He said, "Every one that is of the truth heareth My voice." Pilate's reply to Jesus was, "What is truth?" (v. 38) It is evident that Pilate could not hear the truth, let alone know what it was! Much of the world today is the same way. Many people walk around looking for truth, trying to find reality. Jesus said, "My sheep know My voice and I know them, and they follow Me" (Jn. 10). Those who truly seek truth will find Jesus, and they will hear (accept) His voice. Many people say that truth is a matter of perception, meaning that truth is what a person perceives it to be. That way of thinking is dangerous because so much deception exists in the world today that, in many cases, it's almost impossible to perceive what is *real* (*the truth*), and what is *false* (*a lie*)! That's why we need the Spirit of truth speaking to our hearts.

Jesus said, "For this cause came I into the world, that I should bear witness unto the truth." You and I have the same responsibility to bear witness to the truth.

For every born-again believer, walking in truth is not an option. It is supposed to be our way of life. Not only are we to walk in truth, but we are also to allow the Spirit of truth rule in our lives and affairs. God told the people, through Joshua:

Now therefore fear the Lord, and serve Him in sincerity and in truth: and put away the gods which your fathers served on the other side of the flood, and in Egypt; and serve ye the Lord. (Joshua 24:14)

The verse says to serve God in *sincerity* and *truth*. Jesus said in John 4:23-24:

But the hour cometh, and now is, when the true worshippers shall worship the Father in spirit and in truth: for the Father seeketh such to worship Him. God is a Spirit: and they that worship Him must worship Him in spirit and in truth.

Even our worship is not accepted unless it is in spirit and in *truth*! The truth is, the way we worship corporately is the way we worship privately. The way we pray in public is the way we pray in private. God is not pleased when we try to publicly display worship that is not a part of our private relationship with Him. Even in our prayer life He wants us to be honest. He already knows our true feelings.

Psalms 15 talks about true worshipers. The questions are asked, "Who shall abide in Thy tabernacle? Who shall dwell in Thy holy hill?" The answer is in the next four verses.

He that walketh uprightly, and worketh righteousness, and speaketh the truth in his heart. He that backbiteth not with his tongue, nor doeth evil to his neighbour, nor taketh up a reproach against his neighbour. In whose eyes a vile person is contemned; but he honoureth them that fear the Lord. He that sweareth to his own hurt, and changeth not. He that putteth not out his money to usury, nor taketh reward against the innocent. He that doeth these things shall never be moved. (Psalm 15:2-5)

Notice that verse 2 says, "He that walketh uprightly, and worketh righteousness [justness, honesty, integrity], and speaketh the truth in his heart." In order to abide in His presence, there must be truth in our hearts. Speaking the truth in our hearts is accepting our failures, inadequacies, and short comings, yet knowing that because of Him and His shed blood we can still worship Him. He has provided the way. We don't try to hide anything. We couldn't if we tried!

Verse 3 and 4 talk about our relationships with one another. This is important to our worshiping in truth. We cannot talk badly about one another. We cannot do evil to our neighbor, point the finger at him or put blame on her. We must hate evil and honor those that fear the Lord. We must be men and women who keep our word. We must be men and women of integrity.

Verse 5 talks about our dealings in the area of finance. All that we have belongs to God, including our money. It is to be used wisely, not for selfish gain but for His glory and the building of His Kingdom.

It ends by proclaiming, "He that doeth these things shall never be moved." Truth provides a sure foundation in our worship. Psalm 24:3-5 says it is those who have clean hands and a pure heart who ascend into the holy hill. That pure heart is an honest heart. It goes on to say that this person will receive the blessing from the Lord and righteousness from the God of his salvation.

Look at what Proverbs 12:17-22 has to say about truth.

He that speaketh truth sheweth forth righteousness: but a false witness deceit. There is that speaketh like the piercings of a sword: but the

*tongue of the wise is health. The lip of truth
shall be established for ever: but a lying tongue
is but for a moment. Deceit is in the heart of
them that imagine evil: but to the counsellors of
peace is joy. There shall no evil happen to the
just: but the wicked shall be filled with mischief. Lying lips are abomination to the Lord:
but they that deal truly are His delight.* (Proverbs 12:17-22)

It says, "He that speaketh truth sheweth forth
righteousness." When we speak truth, we are showing the righteousness of God. He is truth. As we
speak truth, we speak forth His ways in the earth.
The word *truth* in this passage comes from the
Hebrew word *emunah*. It means firmness, steadi-
ness, steadfastness, faithfulness, trust, *honesty*
(#530 Strong's).

In verse 19a the passage says, "The lip of truth
shall be established for ever." Truth never changes.
It will last throughout time. When we speak truth,
we are speaking Jesus. He said, "*I am* the way, *the
truth* and the life."

In verse 22b it says, "But they that deal truly are
His delight." The Lord delights in those who walk in
truth, those who walk in His Word. You can not deal
in truth without appropriating the Word of God in
your life. Jesus said in John 17:17, "Thy word is
truth." It is the truth that sets us apart and makes
us different. It is truth that sanctifies us.

Truth also is to be our protection.

He shall cover thee with His feathers, and under His wings shalt thou trust: His truth shall be thy shield and buckler. (Psalm 91:4)

Walking in "the way of truth" is walking in the Word of God, walking in Christ. The protection we then receive is seen in Psalm 91:5-13.

Thou shalt not be afraid for the terror by night; nor for the arrow that flieth by day; nor for the pestilence that walketh in darkness; nor for the destruction that wasteth at noonday. A thousand shall fall at thy side, and ten thousand at thy right hand; but it shall not come nigh thee. Only with thine eyes shalt thou behold and see the reward of the wicked. Because thou hast made the Lord, which is my refuge, even the Most High, thy habitation; there shall no evil befall thee, neither shall any plague come nigh thy dwelling. For he shall give his angels charge over thee, to keep thee in all thy ways. They shall bear thee up in their hands, lest thou dash thy foot against a stone. Thou shalt tread upon the lion and adder: the young lion and the dragon shalt thou trample under feet.

It is a complete covering from the dangers and snares that we often face. Notice in verse 5 it says, "Thou shalt not be afraid." When we walk in truth, we can boldly walk in faith. Yet we not only walk in truth, we also *wear it*!

In Ephesians chapter 6, truth is an important part of our armor.

Wherefore take unto you the whole armour of God, that ye may be able to withstand in the evil day, and having done all, to stand. Stand therefore, having your loins girt about with truth, and having on the breastplate of right- eousness; and your feet shod with the prepara- tion of the gospel of peace; above all, taking the shield of faith, wherewith ye shall be able to quench all the fiery darts of the wicked. And take the helmet of salvation, and the sword of the Spirit, which is the word of God. (Ephes- ians 6:13-17)

It says, "having your loins girt about with truth." In those days, it was the girdle, or the belt wrapped around the waist, that held the garments or armor in place. If that piece was not secure, the person wearing the armor could be injured, or worse. Truth is the piece that holds everything in place.

Remember, Isaiah 59 says:

None calleth for justice, nor any pleadeth for truth: they trust in vanity, and speak lies; they conceive mischief, and bring forth iniquity. ...The way of peace they know not; and there is no judgment in their goings: they have made them crooked paths; whosoever goeth therein shall not know peace. Therefore is judgment far from us, neither doth justice overtake us: we wait for light, but behold obscurity; for brightness, but we walk in darkness. ...In transgressing and lying against the Lord, and departing away from our God, speaking oppression and revolt, conceiving and uttering from the heart words of falsehood. And judgment is turned away backward, and justice standeth afar off: for truth is fallen in the street, and equity cannot enter. Yea, truth faileth; and he that departeth from evil maketh himself a prey: and the Lord saw it, and it displeased Him that there was no judgment. (Isaiah 59:4,8-9,13-15)

"Justice standeth afar off: for truth is fallen in the street." That's where you and I come in. That's where the Church is supposed to hold up the standard. Where there is no truth, there is no justice. That's why the moral fabric of our country is being torn apart! America is in trouble!

We have the homosexuals screaming for rights, the abortion clinics screaming for rights, the music industry screaming for rights, the movie and entertainment industry screaming for rights, every religious cult and occult screaming for rights—but no one is asking for justice! Before you can have justice, you must have truth. Jesus said, "I am the way, the truth, and the life: no man cometh unto the Father, but by Me." (Jn. 14:6) He is the truth! If we are to represent Him in the earth today, we must uphold truth.

In John's epistles, we can see that he placed a great deal of emphasis on truth.

He that saith, I know Him, and keepeth not His commandments, is a liar, and the truth is not in him. (1 John 2:4)

I have not written unto you because ye know not the truth, but because ye know it, and that no lie is of the truth. (1 John 2:21)

But the anointing which ye have received of Him abideth in you, and ye need not that any man teach you: but as the same anointing teacheth you of all things, and is truth, and is no lie, and even as it hath taught you, ye shall abide in Him. (1 John 2:27)

My little children, let us not love in word, neither in tongue; but in deed and in truth. (1 John 3:18)

John is very clear in his writing. He says that if we do not keep the Lord's commandments, then we lie and the truth is not in us. Truth will cause consistency in our walk if we allow it.

Notice also in First John 3:18 he says it is not enough to love in word, but that we must love in deed and in truth. Our actions are what's important. There must be consistency in what we say and do. That's why it's so important for us to not only love God, but also one another. Look at First John 4:20-21:

If a man say, I love God, and hateth his brother, he is a liar: for he that loveth not his brother whom he hath seen, how can he love God whom he hath not seen? And this commandment have we from Him, That he who loveth God love his brother also.

To say we love God and yet hate our brother or sister makes us a liar. Now, you may say, "I don't hate anyone." It is interesting to note, however, that the Greek word used in this case for hate is *miseo*. It means "to detest or to persecute," but it also means "to love less" (#3404 Strong's). If for some reason you make the decision to treat another with *less love* than you previously did, then God says you are *hating* that person. Often we shy away from others, or mistreat or *persecute* them with our "silent treatments" because they told us the truth or because we believed lies others told us about them.

I cannot judge you on this matter, but there is One who knows for sure the conditions of our hearts toward others. If you are having problems with truly loving a brother or sister for whatever reason, confess it to the Lord, for *He already knows*, and ask Him to help you. You see, you may say you love everyone, but God knows by looking at your heart that there are some people you don't love. He says you are lying rather than admitting the truth. Truth produces honest, strong relationships.

The Word goes on to say:

The elder unto the elect lady and her children, whom I love in the truth; and not I only, but also all they that have known the truth; For the truth's sake, which dwelleth in us, and shall be with us for ever. Grace be with you, mercy, and peace, from God the Father, and from the Lord Jesus Christ, the Son of the Father, in truth and love. I rejoiced greatly that I found of thy children walking in truth, as we have received a commandment from the Father. (2 John 1-4)

The Lord rejoices when believers walk in truth. I believe that the Father has great joy when He sees His Body not only hearing the Word, but also walking in the Word—walking in that truth that has been revealed.

Teach me Thy way, O Lord; I will walk in Thy truth: unite my heart to fear Thy name. (Psalm 86:11)

I have a pastor friend who said the greatest compliment any member could give him is to take the Word that has been taught and walk it out, live it out, and apply it to everyday life. That's what John was writing about in his second epistle.

Our nation will not turn around because of the President, the House, or the Senate. It's not up to the Democrats or the Republicans. It's up to the Church—You and me! We are the ones who have the Spirit of truth, and because we have the Spirit of truth, we should be able to speak the truth in love. The Word of God, which is the Word of truth, can not fail us, so we must continue to speak it forth. The Word of God, the truth, has the power to stand against any opposition and conquer it.

This is the hour when God, once and for all, is setting the foundation. This time it will not be shaken or compromised. Those who are rising up have counted the cost and are willing to pay the price to see the Church come forth in power and glory. They have allowed truth to work in their hearts and lives and now they are ready to lay down their lives. Their confession is Galatians 2:20:

I am crucified with Christ: nevertheless I live; yet not I, but Christ liveth in me: and the life which I now live in the flesh I live by the faith of the Son of God, who loved me, and gave Himself for me.

The fear of speaking the truth is gone; the fear of hearing the truth is vanished. The only thing that matters is fulfilling the purposes of God and seeing the Church come to maturity as the Bride of Christ. I believe you are one of those God is calling to stand!

Make a vow in your heart today between you and the Lord. Tell Him:

"Lord, I will stop resisting the Spirit of truth in my life. I will allow the Word of truth to work in my life. I will speak the truth in love. With Your help, I will stand when truth in me is tested. From this moment forward I renounce the way of lying, for I have chosen the way of truth."

I can hear the Father saying:

"I have no greater joy than to hear that My children walk in truth."

Bibliography

Spiros Zodhiates, Th.D., *The Hebrew-Greek Key Study Bible,* Fifth Printing 1988, Copyright 1984 by Spiros Zodhiates and AMG International, Inc., D/B/A AMG Publishers, World Bible Publishers, Inc., Iowa Falls, Iowa.

James Strong, *The Exhaustive Concordance of the Bible,* Peabody, Massachusetts; Hendrickson Publishers, n.d.

About the Author

John W. Stevenson is an associate pastor with oversight of the Music, Worship and the Arts Ministry at Christ Emmanuel Christian Fellowship in Cincinnati, Ohio. John and his wife of 13 years, Marissa, have five children: John, Leslie, Nicholas, David, and Christopher.

In 1980 John founded Heirs International Ministries (H.I.M. Inc.). The focus of H.I.M. is to proclaim the gospel to all the world and to bring people into the presence of God through praise and worship.

In affiliation with Christ Emmanuel Ministries, Inc., H.I.M. is committed to serving the Body of Christ with a cutting edge ministry that will nurture the growth and maturing of all its members. Publications like *Nothing But the Truth* are just extensions of H.I.M., which also includes the following operations: musical recordings, song writing and arranging, dynamic teaching and preaching, a radio and television ministry, and a prophetic praise and worship/music ministry.

In the spring of 1992, John led a team of 12 people, six from the United States and six from Sweden, into Russia to conduct church meetings and outdoor evangelistic street meetings. During this trip God confirmed the apostolic anointing on John as he taught on church government and spiritual authority in local churches. Many were won to Christ and future trips are planned.

John is a writer for Integrity Music, and his songs are recorded by churches and ministries around the country, including Kent Henry Ministries and James Robison Ministry. He has written, arranged, and produced three albums (choir, ensemble, and small group).

With the anointing of God as a multi-gifted musician and psalmist, John leads people near and far into new heights of praise and worship. He also teaches on praise and worship as a life style in seminars, workshops, and conferences around the world. Through John's sensitivity to the Holy Spirit and his commitment to excellence in ministry, many have been challenged and exhorted to a more intimate relationship with God the Father, His Son, and His precious Holy Spirit.

For further information write to:

John W. Stevenson
2828 Vernon Place
Cincinnati, OH 45219
Phone: 513-569-8500